SEVEN SEASONS

on stowel lake farm

Jennifer Lloyd-Karr, Elizabeth Young & Lisa Lloyd | *with recipes by* Haidee Hart

FOREWORD BY **MICHAEL ABLEMAN**

SEVEN SEASONS

on stowel lake farm

STORIES AND RECIPES THAT NOURISH COMMUNITY

PAGE TWO
BOOKS

Cataloguing in publication information is available from
Library and Archives Canada
ISBN 978-1-989025-08-6 (hardcover)
ISBN 978-1-989025-15-4 (ebook)

Produced by Page Two Books
www.pagetwobooks.com

Cover and interior design by Peter Cocking
Cover photography by Rush Jagoe
Printed and bound in Canada by Friesens
Distributed in Canada by Raincoast Books
Distributed in the US and internationally
by Publishers Group West

18 19 20 21 22   5 4 3 2 1

www.stowellakefarm.com

PHOTOGRAPHY CREDITS:
All photos by Rush Jagoe, except:
Stowel Lake Farm archives: pp. 21, 22, 59
Ron Watts: pp. 58, 96 (top) 126, 127, 128, 151, 181 (top),
202, 203, 213, 307
Jen Steele: pp. 61 (top left, top right, bottom left)
Haidee Hart: pp. 71, 90, 271, 316
Syd Woodward: pp. 89, 97 (bottom right), 195,
211, 212, 215, 217
Ashley Casault: p. 92
Paul Shoebridge: p. 130 (bottom)
Jennifer Lloyd-Karr: p. 135
Elizabeth Young: p. 262

We dedicate this book to the uncompromising wisdom of the earth and to the first peoples who knew this land.

CONTENTS

FOREWORD

BY *Michael Ableman*

IN THE EARLY seventies I joined a community based on agrarian principles. We had several pieces of land totalling some four thousand acres on which we raised row crops and had extensive orchards, a cow and goat dairy, and our own natural food stores, juice factory and bakery. Three hundred of us came together to learn to live simply on the land, to farm, to meditate and to work together. It was a grand experiment with skills and lessons that have served me to this day, but in the end the pressures of the world around us and the human challenges of governance and communications forced an unravelling.

For years, I have watched my friends at Stowel Lake Farm work through many of the same challenges I experienced so long ago, and do so with a renewed energy, intelligence and courage that has inspired me and many others living on Salt Spring Island and beyond.

When strangers find out that I have been farming full-time my entire adult life, they sometimes respond with what feels like sympathy, and often with a comment about "the hard work," as if every day is spent bent over in the fields digging ditches.

In fact, the biggest challenges on a farm are not the physical ones—not pests and diseases (we are not, as is commonly thought, like generals out in our fields fighting off some invading force), or weather, or markets, or any of the myriad complexities that come with only two percent of us providing the nourishment for the rest. The real challenges are the human ones—how to get along, work together, live together and respect each other and the land.

This is why the work at Stowel Lake Farm and the model the community there has created are so absolutely essential for us all. Their willingness to engage deeply with one another, to work with and accept individual differences, to deal with the hard personal stuff—all while running a farm that is both beautiful and productive—is remarkable.

The pages that follow tell the story of a group of intrepid individuals who have gone on a journey together. This account is told in the voices of those who live and breathe the daily life, work, land and food of this inspiring enterprise. From its inception to its current incarnation, we hear the wisdom and experience of its gracious elder founder, and insights and recipes from farmers and cooks, mechanics, builders and even the children whose lives have been informed by being raised and nurtured there. The vignettes and stories are light and playful, the connection to the land respectful, the food abundant and beautifully and lovingly prepared and shared.

As we bear witness to enormous political, social and ecological upheaval in the world, it is easy to be overwhelmed by the enormity of our modern dilemma. We know that change is necessary, but it may be that the kind of structural change that is required cannot happen until it has to, until the impacts become local and personal. The hopeful piece is that humans have an incredible capacity for ingenuity, creativity and resourcefulness, especially when under duress or faced with a crisis. There are numerous historical examples of individuals and communities coming together even as the world around them was coming apart.

What is necessary now is that we create, perfect and support these kinds of models, so that when the time comes, there will be places we can seek out for guidance and direction. Stowel Lake Farm is one such place, a true beacon that shows us not only how to nourish the land and our bodies, but how to care for each other as well.

MICHAEL ABLEMAN is a farmer based on Salt Spring Island. He is the author of *From the Good Earth; On Good Land; Fields of Plenty* and, most recently, *Street Farm: Growing Food, Jobs, and Hope on the Urban Frontier*.

WE LIVE ON STOWEL
Lake Farm, a thriving organic
farm and retreat centre on
Salt Spring Island, BC. We are
a community of people living and working
together on the land. Living in community
here is deeply rewarding for all of us, and
it's what inspired us to write this book.
We hope that, as you flip through its pages,
some part of it—the recipes, the stories of
life on the farm, the photos of this place
and its people—will inspire you.
WELCOME!

LISA'S *story*

THE STORY OF Stowel Lake Farm goes a long way back, to my childhood years. I always wanted to farm. When I was a child, we used to go to Kelowna in the BC Interior to stay at my uncle's ranch, and I loved it there. I loved the cows, the horses, the smell of the hay, swimming in the creek—everything about it. My mother took me to another farm just outside Victoria when I was about eight and I remember saying to myself even then, "I am going to live on a farm."

My mother loved nature, and she always encouraged my affection for the land and for growing things. We lived on a beautiful ocean property, with gardens and lots of trees to climb. My siblings and I were outside all the time.

My hunger to live on the land somewhere never left me. In the mid-seventies my then-husband Stuart and I saw that the old Reynolds farm, a 115-acre parcel of land here on Salt Spring Island, was up for sale—and it was affordable. The Reynolds family had cleared the land and logged a lot of it in their early years pioneering here. We loved the property, and though Stuart is himself a farmer now, he didn't want to organize a farm operation here at that time. I really did. Ultimately, we went separate ways, and I remained here raising our three children, Hamish, Rachel and Jennifer.

I tried so many things as a farmer. In the early years I worked with my friend Garry Kaye, who lived with his wife and son down the road. His mother had been born on the farm, and he had happy memories of working here in the summers as a young man, so he was interested in working with me. We bought sixty ewes from Vancouver Island and went to work, building fences and getting fields into production.

The first big challenge with the sheep was the realization that our new ewes had foot rot. We were naive for sure! This condition is difficult because the bacteria that causes it is anaerobic and lives in the soil, so our work was cut out for us immediately. Garry built sterilizing foot-bath troughs that the sheep would run through on their daily rounds, and we checked their feet regularly.

Our life with sheep was full of discoveries, mostly because I really knew nothing. We would read books and talk to neighbours and other people, and gradually we began to understand what was entailed in looking after a flock. There was hay to make for the ewes and all the lambs they delivered every year. We had an old hay baler that broke down a lot; we spent so much of our summers all around the island making hay for the winter months.

In the old days on Salt Spring, a lot of the sheep roamed free on unclaimed lands, particularly in the summertime. This helped with their food needs, and it left the winter pastures available for hay. It also helped with the diseases to which sheep are prone, which is why open pastures really work well for them. Unfortunately our sheep had to be more confined on our parcel of land, and due to their wandering instincts they were always escaping. I would get calls from neighbours saying, "Lisa, your sheep just walked by."

In the spring when the lambs were born, we would bring them down from the hillsides into the barn. At night, they slept in a big pile in the creep, an area the lambs could get into but the ewes could not. We would leave a heat lamp on in the coldest times and they loved it in there. When they were awake and playful, they would run all over the ewes' backs, and in and out of the barn, just exuding that young joy of life.

It was really a time of hard work, learning and wonder. Eventually it changed, as things do. My children were growing up and getting interested in riding, so we transformed the barn into a horse boarding facility for the next number of years. Many children would spend hours in the barn after riding, cleaning their tack and making horse jumps in the middle of the barn. It was lots of imaginative play and preparation for the many shows they started to attend.

Horses need constant care and can't be left on their own. Since I was on the farm every day, I decided to partner with my friend Bruce and get a milk cow, another animal that needs daily attention. Her name was Star and she had to be milked twice a day. She gave so much milk, six gallons a day, and I can remember being totally in tears while learning how to milk that cow. We kept moving her closer and closer to the house to avoid lugging those buckets of warm milk across the property. We put the milk into jars—these were the most spotless and pure objects on the farm—and kept them in a fridge to sell to people on the island.

Strawberries came in after the horses replaced the sheep. I'd heard that strawberries were a mortgage breaker—a rather good way to make money as a farmer—and I still had a sizable agricultural land grant that I needed to pay off. So in the late eighties I put in 12,000 strawberries over a three-quarter-acre piece. I became known on Salt Spring as the strawberry lady. Coming out to our U-pick field or buying them direct from us was a favourite thing to do on the island back then, and every June I spent the whole month in the strawberry patch with the kids, picking and sorting berries. It was really hard work, but there was magic in it, too. In the summers we would all sleep on the veranda, the kids and I, their friends, the cats and the dogs—all of us sleeping outside with strawberries all around.

One of the greatest blessings of those days was becoming a part of the community here on Reynolds Road. There were many fun gatherings on the road. Most of the people were feeling their way into a new way of life, building their houses, growing their own food and raising their children in community. We had some wonderful barn dances, with many community members participating both in the feasting and in the music later.

One thread through all the years was people coming onto the farm for yoga classes and

TOP, LEFT AND RIGHT: The original farmhouse in 1973.
BOTTOM LEFT: Lisa "the Strawberry Lady," circa 1985.
BOTTOM RIGHT: House renovation in the late 1970s.

21

22

FACING TOP, LEFT AND RIGHT: Haying, circa 1985.
BOTTOM LEFT: The Barn in 1985 (built in 1973).
BOTTOM RIGHT: Lisa's children, Hamish, Jennifer and Rachel, circa 1983.

meditation at the old farmhouse, which is where the Gatehouse is now. Yoga on the farm goes back to the early eighties, and later I got into Buddhism and sat with a group of local women. We'd meditate on the veranda of the old house, and I thought it would be lovely if we could have retreats on the farm. As the years progressed, people began coming for the weekend to attend non-residential retreats. It wasn't until my dad died and left me some money that I decided to invest this windfall in the farm's future and build the infrastructure for residential retreats, among other things. This was a pivotal moment for me as many options arose, but I could see how it could develop into something that served those of us on the farm and those in the greater community everywhere. So I took a giant risky leap into the unknown.

INVITING PEOPLE ONTO the land in those days was all part of a strong urge I felt for community, an urge that has been with me as long as I've felt the desire to farm. Stuart and I used to talk about it when living in Victoria and, just as with farming, I'd say, "This is what I want to do with my life. I want to live in a community."

Of course, that word means many things to different people. One year Stuart and I rented an RV and went for a trip into the Okanagan with Hamish, Rachel and Jennifer. On that trip we visited an intentional community started by a friend of ours up near Armstrong and we ended up staying there for two nights. It was a very seventies-type hippie gathering place, and I have a vivid memory of them butchering a roadkill deer on their kitchen table. For most of the time while we were visiting they were all trying to reach consensus about something. Our friend who lived there and had invited us turned out to be the one supporting the whole operation. She was the only one who had a job, paying the bills for all these well-meaning but rather vague people who were sitting around saying, "Well, what do we really want to do?"

Even after that eye-opening experience I still wanted to live in community, but I was starting to get more realistic about what that meant. Most intentional communities that started with very idealistic or opinionated motives didn't last; many of them imploded quite spectacularly. For me, I had no real agenda of what a community should look like. My only real bottom line was that it should be respectful—made of people who are respectful to each other, and to the land—and that the people who lived there should be interested in the common good, not just themselves.

By the early nineties Rachel, Hamish and Jennifer had left the farm. I remained, and everything just limped along for several years. There was always someone living here in a VW bus or in a back room, and they each left their mark in various ways, but there was nothing that felt very cohesive. It was when Jennifer and her friend Liz came back to the farm in the early 2000s, and eventually decided that they would raise their own families here, that Stowel Lake Farm really started to blossom. The Hart family came, Haidee and Josh with their children, and then others who established our current culture—a core of people who care about each other, about farming, and about living in harmony with the land.

If I have any advice about building community, it is perhaps the wisdom of patience, of waiting for things to unfold in the right way. When Jennifer came back, I never said to her, "I think you should stay on the farm," because I didn't really think she ought to. I didn't want her to feel that she should, either, simply because I was here. Many times I thought about selling the farm. I left that door open, but I just didn't seem to be able to leave, mainly because I was in love with the land here. I still am. It has been one of my deepest relationships in life—a real love affair.

So I carried on and waited, through the lonely years after Jennifer had left for school and when my other children were doing their lives, wondering what I was going to do. Now those years feel very important in retrospect. Those times where you're not sure what is going to happen, where you're just holding on barely to a thread of hope that things will work out—I think years like those build up a mysterious form of grace.

I never pressured anybody to stay. I just let it unfold, and it has unfolded so beautifully, in so many ways that I'm grateful for and that I've been astounded by. It was a leap of faith to do so, and what I've learned with everything I've done here is that it isn't about me. That's a real conviction I have: that it hasn't been me really making things happen here. It was the same feeling when I was building the stone wall on the farm. Sometimes you get that inkling that you are simply in the flow of doing what ought to be done, and that what you're doing is part of some movement or necessity that is much bigger than your own impulses.

WHEN IT CAME to telling our story in this book, I was a reluctant debutante. I do love to read, but writing a book was not my first instinct. Over the years, we've been told by so many people that we need to write a book, one that would, among other things, recount how Stowel Lake Farm came to be.

We have really forged our way through some very difficult day-to-day realities, not only around farming but about living in community. While getting here has been such an enormous amount of work on all kinds of levels, it has been a joyful journey. In our world now, we need new ways of being with challenges; we need creativity and commitment. My wish is that this book will reach readers with some alternative possibilities and give them ideas, courage and hope for their journeys.

LISA

JENNIFER'S *story*

I WAS FIVE YEARS old when I moved to the farm with my mum, sister and brother. Everything seemed so big—the drafty farmhouse, the walk to the lake, the fir trees. I spent a lot of my childhood in the now-renovated barn, building stairs out of hay bales and swinging on the giant rope swing right out of the big opening on the front wall. My horse had a stall in the barn, and I practically lived there with my friends and their horses, doing anything and everything horse-related. As I grew up, the whole farm became more familiar and a little less big. Now I see my sons Alex and Rio building their own relationship with different parts of the farm, and they each have special places that resonate for them.

The farmhouse where I grew up is now the Gatehouse, where we host retreat groups. When I spend time in there, welcoming retreat groups, practicing yoga or dancing, it feels so very different, yet still has the same energy it's always had. The view to the west and across the field is the same, and the way the evening sun pours into the Gatehouse reminds me of happy childhood meals on our old porch. I have spent many years on this farm, and have seen and been a part of the enormous change and growth. But the land, the trees, the rocks, the feeling and essence of this farm remain unchanged.

After university I came back to farm during the summers, but I didn't have any long-term plans for building a future here. In my twenties the farm was a place to land before my next adventure, whether that was sea-kayak guiding or travelling in Central and South America. Liz joined me one year and little did I know that this was to be the beginning of a lifetime of working and playing on this farm with her. The fun and joy we shared growing a market garden—learning to save seeds and use a tractor, early mornings harvesting vegetables with our favourite music playing in the truck—kept us coming back and fuelled my commitment to living here, to starting the farm/retreat business, and eventually building a house and raising my family. Luckily for me, my husband David also saw the richness in living here in community, and supported me in choosing this lifestyle.

It hasn't always been easy being so invested in the family farm. Committing to this farm has required me to dig deep into myself, trusting that this is my life's work and growing into who I need to be in this place where I was a child. I've learned so much through the struggles of building a successful market garden and retreat business.

Running the farm business is only half of my life. The other half, or more, is working to build and steward a healthy, functioning community here on the farm. In practice this means spending a lot of time listening to members of our farm community—holding space for them and helping resolve conflicts when they arise. My days are busy with meetings, decisions and time in the office, and they are dynamic and interesting.

It is a great privilege to be at the helm of this big legacy project called Stowel Lake Farm. Working alongside my extraordinary mum and all the wonderful children who are growing up here reminds me that building a multigenerational project is possible. I live this life on the farm and in community because it simply feels right, and there's nowhere else I'd rather be. I get to share time and place with people who encourage me to thrive. My hope is that this farm and this land can continue to hold people to grow and find peace—both people coming for a weekend and people who call the farm home.

JEN

LIZ'S *story*

ONE OF MY favourite things about living on the farm is walking around with my kids on summer evenings. By the time dinner is over, the heat of the day has cooled off and the trees are making long shadows. It's a perfect time to be out on the land. One evening last summer we went out to the fields to prop up the hay bales—something we do in the days after haying, so that they're dry when they get picked up—and once the job was done, we just wandered. Out in the garden we grazed on strawberries, admired the leek flowers that were just starting to bloom and visited the bunnies.

What I love the most about farm life is the possibilities. On walks like this there's the possibility of running into someone and saying hello, of coming across the family of quail that lives in the garden or of just experiencing the familiar landscape somehow in a new way.

I grew up in the city, but from a young age I always wanted to be outside, connected to nature and wild places. In my teenage years and early adulthood I learned about, and eventually began working in, outdoor education and guiding. It was while leading trips as a kayak guide that I met Jennifer. The two of us had an instant connection, and we developed a friendship around our shared sense of humour, our love of doing a job well and our ongoing desire to make things run as effectively as they can. Our friendship eventually led me to the farm, and our ability to make each other laugh while working side by side continues to this day.

Stowel Lake Farm drew me partly because of my friendship with Jennifer, but also because I was interested in learning how to grow my own food—and because I was searching for a more stable existence than guiding. I'd been practicing yoga for a few years and I wanted a place where I could have a more focused and continuous practice.

My first season on the farm I lived in a school bus that sat at the back of the garden. It had been retrofitted into a little home, and though it had no power or running water it was a sweet little space to call my own. My first few years farming were very exciting—so much to learn and do. I knew nothing about farming when I arrived and I was given the opportunity to learn as much as I wanted, from growing healthy plants to driving the tractor to marketing. It was inspiring to join a group of farmers who were as passionate about learning and growing as I was.

Lisa was leading the farm in a very unconventional way, opening it up to—and accepting input from—people like me, who were interested in the farming life but not yet committed. Lisa has a lot of wisdom about letting her vision unfold without being stuck on the details of how everything will happen. I really appreciated that at the time, and I still do. She has turned into a friend and mentor for me. My relationships with Lisa and Jennifer are a big part of why I stayed on the farm.

My husband Matt and I got married on the farm and began to put roots down. We moved into a yurt, where we lived for almost six years and where we had our first two babies, before building a house on the land. A yurt is really just a large, round tent, with a couple of layers of canvas between you and the world. You feel really close to the elements in a yurt. Listening to the frogs sing in spring was incredible, and when it rained sometimes it was so loud that we could hardly hear each other talk, which I absolutely loved.

My role on the farm these days is much different than it was when I first arrived. Jennifer and I are both still passionate about growing things, but we find ourselves out in the fields less and working behind the scenes more: alongside Lisa, we organize on behalf of the community and run the event and retreat side of the business.

A big part of why we do retreats, and why we're writing this book, is to share this amazing place. There is something special about how we are living together, and it continues to be a joy to share it with others, and have their experiences here reflected back to us. Just like wandering on summer evenings with my kids, I love all the possibilities within this shared life we're building together—and the inspiration we hope the farm can bring to others who want to live in community and closer to the land.

LIZ

HAIDEE'S *story*

GREW UP ON the west coast of Vancouver Island, where vast, empty beaches stretch for miles along the edge of the Pacific. I learned as a young child to value wild places, rugged weather and great coastal food. My dad made his living as a logger, which meant living in a lot of remote areas, where fresh fish, game and wild foods were a big part of our diet. He gave me a great love for vegetable-forward cooking, passing down his deep appreciation of simple, fresh foods. I have incredible memories of living on a houseboat in a bay off Haida Gwaii, where my mom and sister and I would dig fresh clams and steam them up for dinner. We often had breakfasts of wild strawberries picked at the forest's edge, and lunches of sautéed chanterelle mushrooms on toast.

I met my husband Josh when I was seventeen. We lived together in a cabin on Brady's Beach in the fishing village of Bamfield, and I learned to improvise with what was on hand or what could be gathered from the wild. We would have huge feasts of freshly gathered oysters and mussels cooked over the fire with friends on the beach.

Over the years this transformed into cooking outside of the home, catering dinner parties, weddings and other special events—and now retreat guests here at the farm. When we first moved to the farm in 2005 I was given the incredible opportunity to work with a team of farmers, rather than trying to grow our food on our own. I now had a supply of fresh greens, heirloom vegetables and fruit coming into the kitchen daily, which propelled me much deeper into the art of seasonal cooking.

The farmers and I see each other at dawn most mornings from early spring to late fall, when nobody else is around the barn kitchen. It's a precious time marked by quick, quiet conversations about what the garden is offering that day. Walking in the fields in the morning to see what's out there is also a great inspiration. I have the great luxury of flexible menu planning, based directly on what is happening in the garden. I can make creative adjustments when a certain vegetable is not ready, or if there is a plentiful supply of something else.

When we first moved here our eldest son, Aliah, was seven, Noah was three and Jacob was just about to have his first birthday. India, our daughter, was born four years later here on the farm, and has really grown up in the barn kitchen with me. The kitchen is the farm's central hearth, a warm hub of creative joy, enticing smells and generous nourishment. It attracts everyone, from kids to farm workers to guests, and there is a constant flow of people and conversation coming through.

The last ten years have been a great journey for me, exploring the world of farm-fresh food within the fabric of a supportive community. We lived next to Lisa for our first thirteen years on the farm, and our relationship has been rich with daily interactions and the love of true neighbours: a cup of milk borrowed, a newspaper picked up in town,

deep caring when tragedies and hard moments have come up. She has been such a tremendous influence on me, modelling the grace and beauty that I hope to embody as I grow older. I watched Jen and Liz become mothers in the early years on the farm and have shared this journey with them: as friends, wives, mothers and businesswomen we have watched each other grow and change so much.

Jen, Liz and Lisa have laid the foundation of the retreat business, which has enabled me to focus almost completely on food. I am very lucky to have such a stable work environment run by women who are so committed to the well-being of the business and the farm. My work overlaps constantly with theirs, and we all benefit from these frequent interactions. We are easily excited and inspired when together, which creates this

incredible energy and I think is a big reason why the farm is doing so well and can hold so much.

My work as a chef on the farm is to create beautiful meals for all those who come here to share this place with us. More and more I lean toward simple recipes that will allow our heirloom vegetables— with their unique structure, bitterness or sweetness, crunch and texture—to really shine. I support artisanal producers locally and beyond, such as small-batch salt makers, ethical meat and egg farmers, and vineyards that value the old traditions of natural winemaking. Sources like these are a big part of the magic that happens in the kitchen. People can taste it in the food, and hopefully they leave feeling inspired to bring some of what they've experienced here into their own homes.

HAIDEE

STOWEL LAKE FARM is over a hundred acres of mixed forests, fields, rocky outcrops and rolling hills. The twenty-five of us who live here have been here for different spans of time. Lisa of course as the founder has been here since the beginning, over forty years ago.

The farm is family-owned, and the rest of us who live here each have our own arrangements for housing. We live together in community but we each have our own homes. Some of us have built houses on the land over the years, almost entirely from wood sustainably harvested on the property, while others live in cabins and yurts.

Over the years we've established meaningful connections with many people who live *off* the farm. They're a diverse group who among other things volunteer their time on Thursdays, participate in our celebrations, are close friends with a lot of us and have developed their own special relationship with the farm.

Within the community there are three families who make up the core group. These families have been on the land since its inception as a community farm in the early 2000s. The core group takes on a stewardship role by facilitating community meetings and events, and working through any big decisions about the direction of farm operations.

Stowel Lake Farm's business operations include our market garden farm and our retreat centre. In the last five years we've received more than 18,000 visitors to the farm through retreats, music events, community gatherings, workshops and farmstand customers.

Both our market garden and our retreat business have grown tremendously in the last two decades. Retreats started informally back in the eighties, when Lisa hosted day-long meditation and yoga workshops. These grew into weekend retreats, and began to really take off with longer residential offerings in 2005. We now host a wide variety of wellness, spiritual and personal development retreats. Yoga, meditation and dance courses, music camps and wilderness-based soul work programs come through the farm every year.

Farming has always been the heart of this place, and our farm team now includes three full-time farmers, one or two apprentices and a host of seasonal volunteers. Together we grow a wide variety of vegetables, fruits and berries that are sold at our farmstand or used for retreat catering. Seed saving is also a big part of our farming, both for our own use and for sale. We sell most of our seeds to Dan Jason of Salt Spring Seeds, and from there they go all over the world. Part of the farm also includes a large permaculture planting on a south-facing hillside that we've cultivated over the last number of years, building a food forest for the future.

The farm is constantly evolving. This book represents our lives right now, in this moment. Constant change keeps things very alive for us; traditions and practices transform or are let go as our needs and desires shift. We have an education program right now that may end when the current group of kids outgrows it. With the ending of something come the space and opportunity for something new to present itself.

LIZ & JEN

EARLY SPRING

IT'S THE MIDDLE OF MARCH, AND ONE OF the first sunny days in weeks. Every day now new life is poking up: the daffodils, crocuses and tulips are making their first bright appearances, and the buds on the huge maple trees are starting to unfurl. The ravens go by high in the sky, carrying sticks for their nests. The hawks are hungry, threatening our laying hens who huddle cautiously in the barn. Our hay is almost gone, and it won't be long before the animals are back out on the land.

You never know with March. Sometimes we can start planting outside, and sometimes it's still too wet, so we work in the greenhouses. Our greenhouse time is vital to our season to come. So much of what we grow has its beginning there. We now have three greenhouses on the farm for starts, transplants and cuttings, and for keeping more tender plants over the winter months.

No matter what the weather is doing, March is a huge month on the farm. Everything outside is coming alive—the miracle beginning once again. Every spring Mother Earth does it once more, and every spring we bow in gratitude.

Pond view with Tamarisk in spring bloom.

The swallows came back yesterday and are swooping around the barn courtyard, exploring the eaves of the village building and the barn, chattering with each other about nests and eggs. Sometimes in the middle of winter's cold and gloom, I think, "Oh goodness, what am I doing here?" Then I read a book about farming or a new seed catalogue, and I remember spring's beauty, its sunny life and the joy of growing things—and the flutter of excitement stirs within. Now the long winter wait is over and the season is shedding its winter coat. We're all feeling a little like the swallows, with those swoops of glory coming through all of us in our own way.

As April comes, the first blush of anticipation will move into fullness, and we'll get to digging up and dividing perennials and doing more to prepare the land for seeding. There's an absolute ton to do around the farm, enough to keep all of us busy from dawn to midnight.

In all of this spring busyness there is the thrill of working together again, the pleasure of being in this with everyone and working toward a common goal. When things are going well, it's the best feeling in the world—a sense of connectedness with each other, with the Earth, and with the tasks themselves that keeps the world, and our little farm, turning in health and harmony.

LISA

OUR FARMING *philosophy*

WHEN WE TALK about where we live, we just call it "the farm." There's a reason: the real act of farming the land is central to our lives here. We talk about the farm, we walk the farm, we admire the farm, we work the farm, we eat the farm. It is us and we are it.

We value our relationships with the people who purchase our vegetables. Everything we grow is sold directly to the consumer, via our farmstand or to Haidee (and other caterers) for our retreats. Most of our customers have some kind of connection to the farm, either from time spent on retreat here or as our neighbours on the island.

Over the years people have come to trust that we make the best decisions we can for the land and the creatures that live here. As an example, summer plantings of certain greens tend to bolt—arugula, mizuna, cilantro—and flower quickly. If planning allows, we like to leave the flowers in the garden instead of pulling them out right away, so the bees can enjoy and feed on them. It's an intentional decision to support the bees. This can go too far, of course: on a couple of occasions we've left the greens up too long and missed our window for planting the next crop!

The farm is an integral whole, a system of relationships between ourselves, the soil, the plants we grow and the forests, fields, birds and animals that surround us. In our decisions—what seeds to buy, what inputs (compost, fertilizer, lime, et cetera) to use, what tools to use or how to manage disease and pests—we try to keep all these interrelated elements in mind. That's how we steward the land, and ourselves, toward sustainability.

Social sustainability is also part of our mission. All too often farmers are overwhelmed, overworked and underpaid. We believe in making farming a viable job and career. We offer our farmers a fair wage, benefits, good housing, time off and a lot of support from our farm community. We want them to thrive and find balance in their lives.

As farmer and author Jean-Martin Fortier put it, we believe in better over bigger. Our market garden is a good size for us to manage. The demand is high for our produce and it can be tempting to grow more and more, but farming about four acres intensively feels sustainable and satisfying for us. To grow more we would need more farmers, a bigger processing area, more tools . . . the list goes on.

We're learning and changing all of the time. So many other farmers out there influence and inspire us, whether they're our neighbours or people halfway across the world. These days, as innovative farmers like Michael Ableman, Eliot Coleman and Jean-Martin Fortier are showing more productive ways to run small-scale organic market gardens, it's essential that we keep on evolving and being responsive to new ideas.

JEN

PREPARING *the soil*

IN MARCH AND APRIL we prepare the soil for planting. We mow down our winter cover crops with a flail mower and leave them to decompose for a week or two. Then we add compost—about a half to one inch—to the top of each bed and top them with a small application of organic, all-purpose fertilizer (many organic, pre-mixed products are available). We form the beds with a power harrow, which, like the flail mower, is an attachment for a walking tractor. Keeping the big tractors out of the gardens helps us maintain the integrity and structure of the soil.

Soil is alive, and we nurture it as best we can so that it will in turn feed our plants. We aim to never have our soil exposed to the elements. In the summer, the soil will dry out and drive deeper the microorganisms and worms that nourish it. In the winter, exposed soil will be eroded and leached of nutrients by the rain. It's a year-round affair. At all times the soil is either planted with crops, covered with mulch or growing a cover crop. This keeps it alive and vital.

We might be ready to prepare our soil in March, but (sadly) it's not up to us. The soil has to be ready to be worked. Each of our gardens has its own relative level of moisture, and spring rains affect each one slightly differently. One way we check is to test a handful of dirt. We can uncover the earth and begin planting seeds only when our handfuls of soil are dry enough to not form a ball. If we've had a wet spring, that ball of earth in our hands tells us we need to wait before preparing the soil. Farming means your plans have to change with the weather. It's a great lifestyle for practicing non-attachment: being attentive to how things are, and not getting too stuck on how you wanted them to be.

JEN

CUT AND COME AGAIN

HARVESTING METHODS BECOME really important when you're producing truck loads of vegetables. "Cut and come again" is one of our favourites. It allows you to get two to four harvests from your herbs and greens, and we've found it works very well for lettuces, cilantro, dill and salad greens (mizuna, kale, mustards, arugula).

Because you're harvesting "baby" versions of these plants, you don't get as much biomass from each seed. Allow one lettuce seed to mature and you get a whole head of lettuce; harvest it early for baby greens and you get a few small leaves. This means you have to plant a lot of seeds to get the amount you need, which is why we tend to use "cut and come again" with crops where we save our own seed.

You start by direct seeding into the garden, close together in rows four to six inches apart. Once the plants are about four inches tall, it's time to harvest them with scissors or a knife, leaving about one inch of the plant to allow it to regrow. When it starts getting hot, the plants may bolt after a couple of cuts without forming a decent third harvest. You know when to stop when the plants start to look poor—small or discoloured, with patchy or uneven growth.

LIZ

THURSDAYS

THURSDAYS ARE OUR community work day, and they're the soul and lifeblood of the farm. We gather every week on that day to work for four hours together and share a lunch. You could show up at 8:30 in the morning wherever our Thursday meeting is being held—Jen's living room in the fall, or out by the greenhouse when it's summer—and say, "Oh, this is just twenty or so people pulling together a work party." And it is that: we do work together on all kinds of jobs that need doing. Weeding the greenhouses, dealing with the recycling, cleaning up the farm room or clearing the forest trails.

But it's also so much more than that. We hold Thursdays, and the day holds our community, in a special way. It's a day we've set aside specifically for the chance to connect, by working and eating together. Doing that is essential to keeping our relationships healthy and alive. Thursdays are also known as Farm Day, and the tradition is such a central part of our lifestyle that some children name the days of the week by saying Monday, Tuesday, Wednesday, Farm Day, Friday, Saturday, Sunday.

Thursdays work really well for us now, but it wasn't always the case. Lisa originally came up with Thursdays as a work trade for people who lived seasonally on the farm. She led and managed them for many years. When the community started to form in earnest in 2005, Thursdays needed to shift, to become much more about working together and connection. At first, we all tried sharing the responsibility of Thursdays while still looking for help from Lisa, and on some Thursday mornings we all stood around awkwardly looking at each other, with nobody really knowing what to do. We quickly realized that being clear and well-organized, and having someone lead it consistently, was essential for the day to be successful and enjoyable.

Liz has been running the Thursday morning meetings for a number of years now. We start every Thursday with an 8:30 a.m. meeting to decide what will happen that day. At that meeting Liz writes the job list on the board and facilitates the process to keep it moving forward and feeling positive. We don't bring major new ideas or issues to Farm Day; big, potentially change-making topics are dealt with through smaller, more focused meetings.

Even this takes some planning: earlier in the week Liz sends out an email with a list of jobs that need to be done around the farm, and we ask people to add to the list. If you want to pull together a successful work party, making a list of most of the jobs that need doing before you meet (and setting the stage with some preparations for the big jobs) is crucial. You don't want to waste half your morning rounding up the tools that you need to get the jobs done!

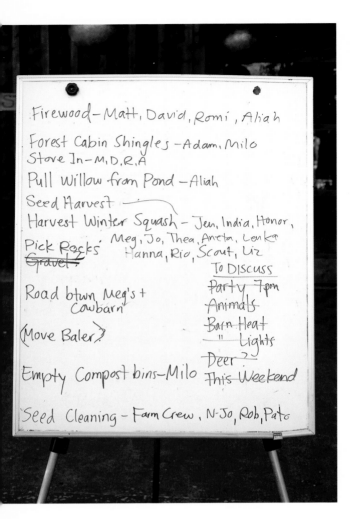

Firewood—Matt, David, Romi, Aliah
Forest Cabin Shingles—Adam, Milo
Stove In—M, D, R, A
Pull Willow from Pond—Aliah
Seed Harvest
Harvest Winter Squash—Jen, India, Honor,
    Meg, Jo, Thea, Aneta, Lenka
Pick Rocks' Hanna, Rio, Scout, Liz
Gravel→
                    To DISCUSS
Road btwn Meg's +   Party 7pm
    Cowbarn   Animals
                    Barn Heat
(Move Baler?)   "   Lights
                    Deer?
Empty Compost bins—Milo This Weekend
Seed Cleaning—Farm Crew, N-Jo, Rob, Pat

Before divvying up job duties, we usually start by discussing any topics that are up that week—animal care, upcoming events, anything we need to make a small decision on. After the discussion of current topics, which usually lasts fifteen to twenty minutes, we run through the list of jobs and everyone signs up. Sometimes our list is far too long to accomplish in one day, and we end up crossing some things off and delaying them until another week.

We always end the meeting with our gratitude circle, which in recent years has actually become the most powerful part of Thursdays. Sometimes people express what's troubling them, but usually it's a chance to share an inspiration or appreciation in the moment. It could be as simple as Felix, one of our young WWOOFers from Germany, saying how the shop and all of its tools are paradise for him, and how happy he is to be able to putter around there and fix machines. Or when Matt says how grateful he is for making dinner while listening to rock music, or Alex says he's thankful for being able to eat handfuls of kale in the greenhouse. Gratitude circles are a vital element of our "social permaculture" on the farm, as is our Thursday lunch—the one meal we regularly share.

Successful shared meals take planning, too. After trying many different ways to run our lunch, we've settled into a system of signing up for soup, salad, bread, dessert or clean-up. There are always little additions here and there that people bring to add to the meal. Our tradition is to invite our elders and guests to eat first. The children love to ring the big bell at lunchtime to call us to gather.

Thursdays are such a part of our farm culture that no one ever asks whether they're happening or not. There might be a Thursday or two during the year when it gets cancelled because it falls on Christmas or something, but other than that, Thursdays happen all year. One time this year when we cancelled our official Thursday because most of us were away, those remaining got together to share breakfast and a gratitude circle anyhow. They said it just didn't feel right to not have that ritual. Rain, shine, dark, light, it doesn't matter. Thursday is always on.

JEN & LIZ

David BROWN

WHEN I FIRST moved to the farm I knew nothing at all about how to be a farmer—not how to work the land, nor how to look after farm animals. In particular, I didn't have a clue about machinery. In the mid-seventies we bought a David Brown tractor, made in England, from an alfalfa farmer up in Westwold, near Kamloops. He's vintage 1965, but we still have David, as we call him. He still gets used each year for haying.

David has quite a few quirks, one of which is a gear that likes to slip out when it gets going. So back in the early days of the farm it was always slightly exciting for me to get on the tractor, even on flat ground. Once I was doing some harrowing on our hillside field, and as I was coming down the hill after making a turn at the top, the gears slipped again and the tractor took off downhill, hellbent for leather—and instead of doing something practical (trying to turn uphill, for example) I just leaped off David and let him crash straight into the fence at the bottom of the field. The fence bent, but luckily for me, nothing broke. Nobody was hurt and life went on.

Garry often laughed about what a farmer I was, and so did I. Life was like that for me in the early years. There was so much to learn about farming, about the land and about country ways.

LISA

FACING: Josh with our beloved David Brown tractor.
RIGHT: Garry Kaye driving David Brown, circa 1983.

EASTER *traditions*

W E HOLD CELEBRATIONS on the farm in a pretty relaxed way. They aren't rigid. We do a lot of the same traditions each year, but we're not sticklers about doing the same thing year after year—at least not us adults! The kids are often far more concerned that we stick to tradition.

For years we've done an Easter treasure hunt for the kids on the farm. Lisa makes up clues that lead them all over the farm. The older kids lead the group, reading clues to the younger ones, and then everyone tries to figure out the answer. Some of us adults will usually tag along, and it's another way we can get out on the land together, wandering from garden to field to barn as a group, which is something we don't get much of a chance to do.

One year we didn't have it together. We hadn't written up the clues, and we had no treasures to find. Easter rolled around and the kids were so excited: "Where's the treasure hunt?" they asked. "When are we starting?" And we all turned to each other with expressions that said, "Oh right, the treasure hunt! We better figure something out, quickly."

Coming up with treasures for the hunt without buying more candy is always a challenge. Last year we gave all the kids a trowel. When they followed the clues and came upon this unceremonious box of little shovels, they weren't sure what they were looking at. "Is this the treasure?" they asked each other. They were a little shocked at first, but they did end up all loving their trowels.

Easter trees are a beautiful tradition that Haidee brought to the farm, and a great way to bring fresh spring energy into the house. Last year I decided I wasn't going to do an Easter tree, and my son Alex went to Lisa and said, "Granny, we need to make an Easter tree, because Mama's not doing it this year!" And so they did: he got the branch and they dyed the eggs, and he put it all together. It was fantastic.

JEN

NATURAL EGG DYEING
and easter trees

Naturally Dyed Eggs

Natural dyes are easy, and the materials are commonly found: red cabbage, coffee, onion skins, turmeric, beets. The results are truly beautiful. Our chickens lay eggs that are various shades of brown, and this is mostly what we use for dyeing. We've found that all of the egg colours work, including white, and each lends its own variation to the dye.

First, wash one to two dozen eggs with soap and water. If you are dyeing your eggs for an Easter tree, you need to blow your eggs first. Take a large needle and poke a hole in each end of the egg (about the diameter of a spaghetti noodle, or a little larger). Put one end of the egg over a bowl and, from the other end, blow the inside of the egg into the bowl. Once all the eggs are empty, rinse them and let them dry in an egg carton, or anywhere they'll stay safe and unbroken.

Blown eggs float, so you need to figure out a way to submerge them in the dye. A plate or some other flat object works to weigh them down. Using a French press works very well too. Submerge the eggs for six to twenty-four hours, depending on the intensity of colour you want.

You can also create beautiful designs on the eggs by placing natural materials (leaves, cedar fronds, grasses, flowers) on the egg and wrapping it with cheesecloth or nylon stocking before placing it in the dye.

Dye Preparation

For all dyes, start by filling a medium pot with water and adding ¼ cup of white vinegar.

Reddish Brown: Onion skins Remove the outer skins from 5 medium to large onions and submerge the skins in the pot. Bring the water to a boil and then simmer for a few hours, or until the water has a deep orange colour, and then strain.

Blue: Red cabbage Roughly chop up half a red cabbage and add it to the pot. Bring it to a boil and simmer for a few hours, or until the water looks dark with colour, then strain.

Pink: Beets Roughly chop 3 to 4 medium-sized beets and add them to the pot. Bring to a boil and simmer for a few hours, or until the water looks dark with colour, then strain.

Yellow: Turmeric Add 4 tablespoons of turmeric to the pot and stir. Bring to a boil and simmer for a few hours, or until the water looks dark with colour, then strain.

Brown: Coffee Make a pot of very strong coffee. Done!

Purple: Blueberries Place 1 cup of blueberries in the pot. Bring to a boil, then let cool and strain.

Green: Mix your dyes Mix the cabbage (blue) and turmeric (yellow) together in equal parts.

Other colours Experiment with other things in your kitchen and garden and with other colour combinations—you never know what might happen!

JEN

63

Q&A: *milo*

MILO'S ROLE IS essential to keeping our farm systems functional and running smoothly. He takes care of so many things, from troubleshooting physical infrastructure problems to sourcing piglets to designing new farm buildings. He's often out on his own, continually educating himself as he works by listening to podcasts under his hearing protection.

Milo spent his high school years splitting his time between family here on Salt Spring and in Grand Forks in southern BC. A scuba diving instructor as well as a sailor, he lived on a 35-foot sloop in the South Pacific for several years. He lives with his partner, Ashley, his two children, Aurelia and Alden, and a lovely big, black dog named Sirius.

What's your favourite thing about your work?

I like problem solving. Being able to get something done, seeing it done well, and knowing I'm not going to have to come back to fix it. I live for that. Since I came here in 2014 I've replaced the entire lake irrigation system. That was about 3,000 feet of big pipe and everything that came off it. The old pipe, which was made of brittle PVC, was full of leaks.

I had help in that job from a guy who had a big backhoe. Quick little construction jobs, though—electrical or plumbing fixes, or digging a drainage trench—I love being able to do jobs like that myself and not having to call in an expert. But when they're here, electricians or plumbers, I like to peek over their shoulder and learn what I can.

You're on your own a lot in your job. Are there ways you feel supported by the community in what you do on the farm?

Thursdays are super important. Sometimes I'll miss a Thursday and it doesn't feel good. It's that time where you get to be with other people, and even if you don't talk much, you get to say your little bit. That's critical, especially when I'm living here on the farm now. I'm a newcomer still, but I'm more than an employee. It's really nice to have that one day a week, too, where I get to work on something that's not on my list, with other people.

What's the deal with eating food made for apes?

I found myself working long hours and late nights last year, and I was having a hard time feeding myself three square meals a day. I have a dog, and there's food for dogs, so as I was pouring it out one day I thought there should be something like that for humans—a whole food you can just eat. It seemed like a pretty good business idea: Sapien Food. I asked myself what was the closest animal to humans, and I ended up ordering a twenty-kilogram bag of Primate Diet Dry.

It tasted a bit like Shreddies cereal. I kept a container of it in my truck as a snack, and just to see what would happen I went a whole week eating nothing but that. And I felt great. I also tried grinding it up in the coffee grinder to make flour for crackers, adding rosemary and eating it with cheese. The best was a little bit of chocolate.

I ended up eating it all. I still think it's not a bad idea.

The beauty of this dish relies on two simple ingredients; fresh, crisp radishes and the best butter you can find. If possible try to source grass-fed butter; this is getting more readily available in shops and farmers markets these days, and is worth looking for. If grass-fed is not available then a good quality unsalted, organic butter can be used. The better the butter, the more incredible this dish will be. SERVES 4 TO 6

RADISHES *with butter*

Clean radishes well, leaving the nice vital greens attached and discarding the rest. Clean and trim the radish root; I like to leave a bit of the root on to keep the whole vegetable intact in all of its beauty. Leave smaller radishes whole, cut larger ones in half lengthwise.

Spread butter to an even thickness on one end of a wooden board or platter. Arrange radishes with their greens at other end of board. Sprinkle butter with sea salt and lemon zest, then arrange herbs and flowers over the surface of the butter.

To serve, encourage guests to dip radishes right into the butter, savouring the smooth creaminess of the butter with the fantastic flavour and texture of the fresh radish.

250 grams high quality unsalted butter, room temperature

Pinch sea salt

Fresh herbs such as thyme leaves/blossoms, chives or chive blossoms and edible flowers to garnish

2 to 3 bunches freshly harvested radishes with greens attached

Finely grated zest of 1 lemon

Our farmers work hard to produce a really great salad blend, which our island neighbours all come to buy at our farmstand. It's a luscious, texturally rich salad with an ever-changing range of colour—the lightest greens through to dark green, red and purple. Right now we're in love with the frilly purple mustards, which add a gorgeous light crunch and beautiful colour.

about SALAD

I like to add a lot of fresh herbs and edible flowers to salads to give extra magic and depth of flavour. For herbs I will cut bunches of freshly picked chives into a salad or put in whole basil or mint leaves, lemony sorrel, wild chickweed, parsley, dill and lemon balm ... the possibilities are endless. Some of my favourite edible flowers are golden calendula, rose petals, purple chive blossoms and the jewel-toned nasturtiums that self-seed throughout the garden each year. Before serving or adding dressing, it's really important to take the time to carefully go through your salad greens to ensure they are all clean, fresh and beautiful.

We have included three of our favourite dressings here. They're packed with flavour and easy to make. We also love a simple drizzle of high-quality olive oil and a squeeze of lemon or splash of good vinegar to dress our salads— especially the first salads of spring when the flavours of the greens and herbs are so delicate.

green salad DRESSINGS

Spring Herb Dressing

2 cups fresh herbs (parsley, dill, etc.)

1 cup apple cider vinegar

1 cup water

¾ cup miso

1 cup extra-virgin olive or sunflower oil

MAKES ABOUT 4 CUPS

Spring Herb Dressing

This is a very flexible and versatile dressing. In the winter and early spring, I make it using just parsley; as the seasons change and we have a larger variety of fresh herbs, I will add cilantro, basil, dill and/ or chives along with the parsley. You can combine different herbs to find the flavour profile that you love. If you use the basic foundation measurements, you can't go wrong and it's always delicious.

Blend all ingredients except oil. With blender running on medium, slowly add oil. Keeps for 2 weeks if kept refrigerated.

Jennifer's Vinaigrette

This wonderful vinaigrette is a big hit at our Thursday lunches. It has a perfect balance of flavour: maple syrup adds a touch of sweetness to complement the bitter and tart flavours of freshly harvested spring greens.

Finely mince garlic. Put garlic and salt into a jar with a tight-fitting lid. Add apple cider vinegar and mix to combine. Add maple syrup, oil and optional mustard. Put lid on jar and shake well to emulsify. Will keep in fridge for 2 weeks.

Best-Ever Tahini-Yeast Dressing

This dressing originated from the Hollyhock Retreat Centre on Cortes Island, BC, just up the coast from us. They have a tremendous cookbook called *Hollyhock Cooks*, which I always recommend highly to our visiting guests.

We have created a version of their great dressing that has a lot of tahini added, making it rich and creamy. Almost every retreat guest asks us about this dressing recipe, so here it is! I think everyone loves it in part because it really hits the spot nutritionally—it's super high in vitamin B from the yeast. It goes really well with a salad of summer greens, right through to the hearty greens of fall and winter.

Blend all ingredients except oil. With blender running on low, slowly add oil until thick and creamy. Keeps well for 2 weeks in the fridge.

Jennifer's Vinaigrette

4 cloves garlic
(about 2 tbsp chopped)

2 tsp sea salt

2 tbsp maple syrup

½ cup apple cider vinegar

½ cup sunflower oil

½ cup extra-virgin olive oil

2 tbsp grainy mustard or Dijon mustard (optional)

MAKES ABOUT 2 CUPS

Tahini-Yeast Dressing

½ cup nutritional yeast

½ cup apple cider vinegar

½ cup tamari or Bragg's or ⅓ cup soy sauce

½ cup water

⅓ cup tahini

1½ cups extra-virgin olive oil

½ cup parsley (optional)

MAKES ABOUT 4 CUPS

There are a few things in my kitchen that I hold with extra reverence; salt is one of them. I am forever talking to people about "good salt" and "good olive oil" because I really believe these are foundational to good cooking.

about SALT

Salt is often seen only as a flavour enhancer, but the minerals it contains—potassium, iron and zinc—are also important to our health. In the last few years there has been a resurgence of artisan salt makers who are honing their craft, learning from ancient salt harvesting traditions while incorporating modern processes and technology. Here on Salt Spring we have a talented salt maker who evaporates, sifts and hand-packs fresh sea-salt—from the beautiful fleur de sel we use for finishing our dishes to more complex salts using blackberries, jalapenos and even beer to add colour, fragrance and flavour.

When I support these small-scale salt makers I feel I'm connecting more deeply with the world of "real food." This is the world in which we know where our products are from, how they're made, and hopefully the person or people behind the making, growing or harvesting. As we veer away from mass production, our food seems to have a gentler, more meaningful quality to it. This style of sourcing proves that simple food is beautiful and exciting, and that it doesn't need to be complicated and time-heavy.

Tortilla soup is the perfect, warming dinner for early spring. I often make it if someone in our house is not feeling well—it has all of the same wonderful healing qualities as traditional chicken soup. The foundation is a flavourful stock made with a whole organic chicken, to which we add slow-roasted tomatoes sautéed with fragrant chili. SERVES 6 TO 8

tortilla SOUP

Chicken stock

1 large whole free-range organic chicken (4 to 5 lb)

10 to 12 cups water

1 tsp whole black peppercorns

3 bay leaves

2 medium onions

Soup

5 onions

2 tbsp Mexican chili powder

2 cups slow-roasted tomatoes (see page 186)

2 tbsp extra-virgin olive oil

1 tbsp salt

12 6-inch corn tortillas

Additional toppings

2 limes

¼ medium green cabbage

2 cups cheddar or Monterey jack cheese

2 to 4 ripe avocados

The addition of some or all of the optional toppings turns this soup into a satisfying meal. The tortilla strips are essential. (In a pinch you can use quality tortilla chips in place of the strips.) For a nice wine accompaniment, try a fruit-forward, low-tannin tempranillo.

Chicken stock Cut onions in half, leaving skin on. Place chicken, peppercorns, bay leaves and onions into a large pot. Add water, making sure chicken is covered by at least 2 inches. Bring to a boil over high heat, then lower heat to a simmer until chicken is cooked through (about 45 minutes).

Carefully pour through a colander into a bowl, reserving broth and setting chicken aside to cool. When chicken is cool enough to handle, remove as much meat as you can from the bones and set aside.

Soup Thinly slice onions into half moons and cut tortillas into ¼-inch strips. Heat oil in large pot over medium heat. Add sliced onions and sauté until golden. Add chili powder, roasted tomatoes and salt. Sauté for 15 minutes until fragrant. Add reserved chicken broth and blend until smooth with immersion blender. Add reserved meat from the chicken. Simmer for another 30 minutes. Add salt and pepper to taste.

Heat 2½ inches of vegetable oil in a deep pan over medium heat until very hot. To test the heat, add a tortilla strip; it should bubble and rise to the top right away when the oil is hot enough. Add tortilla strips and fry carefully until light golden brown and crisp. Remove to a plate covered with paper towel and salt lightly.

Additional toppings Shred the cabbage finely, grate the cheese, dice the avocados and cut the limes into quarters. Place these additional toppings into condiment bowls for people to add to their own bowl of soup.

Some of the first abundant spring vegetables on the farm are radishes and turnips. They are colourful and wonderful to eat raw (French style with butter and salt—yum!) and they become quite decadent when roasted on high heat until tender. SERVES 4 TO 6

ROASTED RADISHES
and turnips

I like to combine multicoloured radishes (pink and purple along with traditional red), along with any small turnips you can find. The white Japanese turnip varieties are lovely, and there are some gorgeous purple-topped ones out there too. Feel free to combine varieties or just use one. Also, I like to leave the tops on. They're tender and get deliciously crispy when roasted. Whether you harvest your own or buy bunches of radishes from the market, be sure to give the radishes a good scrub and the greens a good rinse.

Miso butter Melt butter in small pot, whisk in miso and maple syrup until smooth. Remove from heat.

Roasted vegetables Heat oven to 425°F. Cut radishes in half length-wise, keeping greens attached if possible. If any greens detach, simply add to the tossing bowl.

Toss radishes and/or turnips with oil and salt in bowl to coat thoroughly. Spread on parchment-lined baking tray and bake for 20 to 25 minutes—until they're tender and turning golden brown and the greens are getting crispy. Remove radish and turnips from oven, toss with miso butter. Return to oven for approximately 5 more minutes until bubbling and golden.

Enjoy hot or add them cold as a great topper on your fresh spring salads.

Miso butter

2 tbsp unsalted butter

2 tbsp miso

1 tbsp maple syrup

Roasted vegetables

3 bunches radishes and/or turnips (about 2½ to 3 lb), greens attached

2 tbsp extra-virgin olive oil

1 tsp sea salt

Rhubarb is a real treasure from the garden. Here on the farm it is one of the first spring plants you can harvest, and after a cold, dark winter its lovely, hot-pink colour is a welcome sight. The roasted rhubarb in this recipe becomes mellow and delicious, and can also be served with a savoury dish, such as a cheese platter or roast chicken. SERVES 8

PAVLOVA *with roasted rhubarb compote*

Roasted rhubarb
2 lb rhubarb
1 cup sugar

Pavlova
4 egg whites
1 cup sugar
1 tsp vanilla
1 tsp cornstarch
1 tsp white vinegar

Sweetened yogurt cream
1 cup thick Greek-style yogurt
500ml heavy cream
1 tbsp sugar
Zest of 1 orange (optional)

Once you get the technique down, pavlovas are light, airy, and extremely versatile. You can top them with almost any seasonal fruit—fresh raspberries, strawberries, blueberries or sliced peaches.

Roasted rhubarb Heat your oven to 350°F. Cut rhubarb into 1-inch lengths and arrange in a 9 × 12-inch baking dish. Sprinkle with sugar and if desired combine with optional orange zest. Bake until soft (about 45 minutes). Set aside to cool.

Pavlova Heat oven to 250°F. Combine vanilla, vinegar and cornstarch in a small bowl and set aside. Beat egg whites in a mixer on medium until stiff peaks are forming. Slowly add sugar while you're still mixing. When all the sugar has been incorporated, gently stir in the vanilla, cornstarch and vinegar mixture.

Line a large cookie sheet with parchment. Using a spoon, divide meringue mixture into 8 equal portions on tray, pushing down gently with back of spoon to create an indentation in each pavlova where the fruit and cream will go once baked. Bake for about 90 minutes, until light golden-brown and firm to the touch.

Sweetened yogurt cream Whip cream until soft peaks have formed. Gently combine whipped cream, yogurt and sugar. To serve, place a small scoop of yogurt cream on each meringue and top with roasted rhubarb.

"Here on the farm
rhubarb is one of the
first spring plants you
can harvest, and after
a cold, dark winter its
lovely, hot-pink colour
is a welcome sight."

HAIDEE

Pavlovas are light, airy, and extremely versatile. You can top them with almost any seasonal fruit—raspberries, strawberries, blueberries or sliced peaches.

LATE SPRING

LATE SPRING STARTS WITH LIFE BURGEON-
ing all around us. Everything in the outside world is greening
and growing. I think of this time as the green pulse of May. Dylan
Thomas expressed so well the sense of these days in his famous
words, "The force that through the green fuse drives the flower."
The riot of new life takes us over and away we go with this new energy.

As growth erupts all over the farm, out come the hoes and the
clippers and the lawn mower. We get to reap rewards after the long
winter wait: salads of spinach and lettuces and arugula, the irises and
tulips and alliums bursting into colour. Now purple and white share
the stage with green.

The greens have held the limelight for some time—it's surprising there are no other names for green in the English language like there are for snow in the Inuit world. The lime green of Euphorbia wulfenii stands out against the grey green of rosemary, the yellow green of berberis and the dark green of other shrubs. It has been a marvellous show.

The first beets and carrots arrive in early June, along with flowering perennials such as nepeta and flowering herbs. Lady's mantle overflows the pathways and all the various peonies announce the lush arrival of June. We're also surrounded by the fragrances of this time of year: the sharp, sweet smell of snowball viburnum and all the aromas of the climbing and rambling roses on the big stone wall.

I walk through the garden every day just to experience all the beauty—appreciating the gifts of the lengthening light and the landscape as it moves toward summer solstice.

LISA

SEEDING *success*

FARMERS KNOW HOW important it is to achieve strong and even germination of their seeds. For beginning gardeners, learning a little bit more about seeding can go a long way. If you can understand and apply some basic germination principles, your garden harvests will increase, and with them your satisfaction and inspiration to keep going!

Whether we're seeding into a flat in the greenhouse or into garden soil outdoors, the measure of successful seeding is a high rate of germination that happens at the same time—all those hopeful little plants must poke their heads through at approximately the same moment, or your crop will be delayed, inconsistent or just a straight-up failure. In early spring we check every day, waiting to see an even line-up of green against the soil that means the seeds have germinated without gaps.

As an added note, we practice succession planting—meaning we don't just germinate once and harvest once. It might seem crazy at the time, but even when your garden is overflowing with abundance and you think you'll never be able to eat it all, you need to be thinking about preparing your next planting. We plant salad greens over twenty times throughout the year, and carrots seven times, along with many other vegetables and herbs, to give us a continual harvest through most of the year (except in deep winter).

The principles of successful seeding apply to all the ways you can do it—by hand, with a seeder, in a tray or outside. Just remember these three words: consistency, consistency, consistency. Seeds thrive on it.

Depth: A general rule is to plant at a depth of four times the seed's shortest dimension. Seeding too deep can result in a delay in germination or may lead to rot, and seeding too shallow can lead to seeds that dry out too quickly.

Even Beds: Bed surface can have a huge effect on germination timing—fortunately, it's one of the easiest factors to control. Smoothing out an even, flat bed helps keep your seeds at a consistent depth so that plants will emerge around the same time. If you are seeding flats inside, you can smooth the bed surface with your hand. (We have a little piece of wood that has lived in the greenhouse for years; we use it for this and many other things.) Outside, this can be done with skillful use of the back side of a rake.

Moist Soil: Seeds need consistent moisture. It helps to be working with healthy soil—soil containing a good amount of organic matter. Most potting soils that contain peat work well. If you're working outside, adding compost will help balance out soils that are either too sandy or have too much clay. In cool months, watering in the late afternoon or

evening can cause the soil to be too cold overnight and may lead to rot and poor germination. In the hot season, we use floating row cover on a freshly seeded bed to keep the seeds from drying out.

Viable Seed: Seeds have a shelf life! Make sure your seed is still good before you start. Storing seeds properly—somewhere cool, dark and dry—is critical for viability year to year.

Soil Temperature: Most seeds germinate best with soil temperatures between 15 and 30 degrees Celsius (60 to 85 degrees Fahrenheit). We use a couple of different strategies when it's cold. Inside we use a heater or heating pad, and outside we use floating row cover like a Reemay garden blanket to hold in warmth.

LIZ

89

THREE *easy herbs*

OUR THREE FAVOURITE herbs that we harvest continuously throughout the growing season are dill, cilantro and parsley. All of these can be grown successfully in a pot outside.

Dill & Cilantro

Dill and cilantro are both quick crops. They're easy to plant and tend, but they need to be seeded in succession for continuous harvest. We start planting in March, seeding rows into our greenhouses. As it begins to warm up—usually near the end of March or in early April—we start planting these outside, and do so until early September when we return to greenhouse planting for harvesting through the autumn. We plant in cut-and-come-again style (see page 53) every two to three weeks, and usually get three cuts off one seeding.

We regularly use our dehydrators throughout the season to preserve the summer's harvest. Home-dried dill is so easy, flavourful and gratifying to have as part of your kitchen. Once a season, do an extra-large planting of dill, then cut it all down and lay it out in a dehydrator—or bunch it loosely and hang it somewhere dry and warm over several days. When ready, rub it gently between your hands and then store the dill in a jar.

The most difficult time for managing dill and cilantro is through the summer, when it's hot and they both want to bolt—sending up a central stalk to form flowers and go to seed. You may only get one or two cuts before the heat takes over and the plants have had enough. Persevere with succession planting of fresh seeds, making sure they get plenty of water.

Parsley

Parsley will grow wonderfully in a pot outside your door for easy harvest, and you can plant it abundantly in your garden. Unlike cilantro and dill, you only need to plant parsley once, early in the season, which for us is late February or early March. Then you get to harvest off the same plants the whole year. Parsley is slightly more difficult to germinate, and takes a long time to come up relative to cilantro and dill. Parsley will germinate within a large temperature range (5 to 32 degrees Celsius) but when we seed in February the temperatures are still quite cool, even with our little heater in the greenhouse. Germination can take ten to twenty-five days, which is a really long time to wait and always causes us some concern.

Start your seeds inside. After six to eight weeks, when the plants are two to three inches tall, transplant them into the garden. Let them grow to at least eight inches tall before you harvest. Parsley plants are hardy and bear well under continuous harvest, as long as you let half of the stalks remain. We like to have enough plants in the garden to be able to do big harvests without depleting them. Parsley is affected by carrot rust fly, so we cover it with floating row cover (see more about pests on page 168).

LIZ

ANIMAL *shares*

W E'VE RAISED CHICKENS on the farm for many years and also have had, off and on, milking cows, beef cows, pigs, rabbits and llamas. Keeping animals on a farm is a lot of work, and we've always found ways to share the responsibility.

When I was growing up, my mum, Lisa, bought a big, beautiful Jersey cow named Emily. She shared the purchase with Craig, a friend who lived up the road. He would come milk, feed and care for Emily half the time. As a young girl I loved sitting on the kitchen counter chatting about life with Craig as he processed the milk. The farm wasn't a community then, per se, but was always a place for sharing projects like a cow or a flock of sheep.

Today we raise food animals for the people living here on the farm, but not as part of our business operations or for off-farm sales. Gradually we've evolved a new sharing system: individuals

(or families) have the option to buy shares in each animal, proportional to their interest in meat or eggs. It's a cost-recovery system, with all shareholders together footing the bill for buying, feeding and processing the animal.

As with any system, somebody needs to be in charge of it, and Milo takes on the responsibility of finances, feed orders and animal sourcing, among other tasks. This is the best approach we've found—it allows us all to participate in raising animals without having to stay home every weekend to feed and care for them.

One of my favourite stories of having animals is about one of our previous head farmers, Sashah, and his attempt to educate some piglets.

We bought two Berkshire piglets one year from a farmer on Vancouver Island. They were maybe two months old. The idea was that they would rotate through the gardens, clear plant material, dig up roots, help with pests and fertilize along the way.

We set up their first area in one of our gardens that had been planted with a cover crop of rye and vetch over the winter. These crops needed to be turned into the soil along with some weeds so that we could plant the garden later in the season.

We brought the pigs home, set them gently in the field and stood back to eagerly watch them work their magic. I'm not quite sure what we were expecting, but these little pigs were not up to the task of digging up this garden. They sniffed around and nibbled the rye a little bit. That was about it.

Sashah thought that maybe these piglets, without their mother's example, didn't know what they were supposed to be doing—that they didn't actually know how to root around and dig up the earth. He figured he was their mother now. So he took action.

He stepped over the low wire to join the pigs, got down on his hands and knees and started nosing the ground with his face. He would look at the pigs, and then dig around in the earth using his nose and chin. The pigs just stared at him. We were in hysterics.

When Sashah got out of the garden, he was literally covered head to foot in dirt. To this day I'm not sure if the pigs learned anything from Sashah or if they just needed to get a bit bigger to be able to really dig up the earth, because they did end up figuring it out as they got older.

JEN

THE WALL

I ALWAYS WANTED THE area between the old farmhouse and the barn to look like a land of milk and honey. That was the way I said it in the early years—and what I meant was that I deeply wished for beauty to replace the barren farm fields that were there when we moved onto the farm, and for many years after. When the opportunity arose to actually do something about it, I felt a strong desire to build a wall between the planned garden area and the rest of the farm. Both areas were equal in importance and so to create a boundary between the two, the idea of the wall was born.

I found two great stonemasons—Andrew Currie, a Scotsman, and Tom Regal, an American from Colorado—who had made their homes on Salt Spring Island. Tom brought his daughter, Ramona, along, and she did all the filling in this dry stone wall, spending hours and hours fitting small stones into the chinks in the wall. We found all the rocks for this project on the island. Tremendous amounts of them arrived in trucks, and made huge piles in the fields around. People on the island came by and laughed, and asked me if I was building the Great Wall of China. It was a destination for a while as people brought their friends by to see it.

And so the wall was born. I've never regretted the decision I made to do this project, and in a way I felt as if I hadn't made a decision at all. It seemed to come through me from the land itself, and it has always felt right—as if it asked to be built.

LISA

I lived as part of the Stowel Lake Farm community for three years, and I am still included in many of the farm's seasonal celebrations. The land and the people there have been a huge part of my personal growth and learning. I feel part of something on the farm, and I deeply appreciate the connection to the land and the multigenerational aspect of the community. In my opinion, this is what we need to return to if we wish to thrive as a culture.

ASHLEY

Since landing in Canada from Colombia and walking through the gates of the farm for the first time eight years ago, I can say that it is one of my favourite places on the planet. To me, Stowel Lake Farm is home. It fills me up, it makes me dream and it reminds me of what's important. I am so grateful for their vision, the hard work that goes into the farm and the incredible people who fill it with life.

ISELA

NATURE *tables*

WHEN I SPEND time outside, alone or with my family, I will often bring home items that have caught my eye along the way—a particularly beautiful leaf or stone, peeling bark, shells, a piece of wood or bone.

Laying out items like this in some simple, decorative way in our homes is what we call a "nature table." They can reflect seasonal changes or celebrations like Thanksgiving, or be souvenirs of family adventures.

Recently, our family went on a week-long kayaking trip to Kyuquot Sound with another family. While camping on a beach on Spring Island, we created a nature table on a driftwood log. Everyone contributed items throughout the week, and by the end it was a beautiful collection of abalone and crab shells, beach glass, bird bones, eagle feathers, stones and driftwood that told the story of our time and adventures together. When we left we returned it all to the sea (minus a few treasures).

Something happens when a collection of found items has been put together with intention. Creating nature tables at home, where they remind us of the world beyond our walls, is especially powerful. Fir cones, feathers, leaves, stones—all of these and so many other things can be mementos of the beauty and perfection of nature.

You can't go wrong with nature tables. They are best however you want them to look. As displays, they're creative and fluid, and can be added to whenever there's inspiration. When the items start looking old, or have been around for a while, I know it's time to return them to the earth and bring new things in. Keep the nature table fresh and full of what is alive for you at the moment.

JEN

Q&A: *meghan*

Being the head farmer is a lot of responsibility. There's a lot to manage, including choosing varieties and overseeing a constant flow of succession planting, weeding, irrigating and controlling the pests—not to mention harvesting it all, and prepping the beds for winter when autumn comes. The head farmer is also responsible for managing the farming team and hiring seasonal employees and apprentices.

With so much to oversee, farming has to be a labour of love. That's true for our head farmer, Meghan, who came to us four years ago. Meghan grew up in southwestern Ontario but the West Coast seems to have won her heart, and her love of growing things runs deep in her bones. She's dedicated her life to organic farming, and she's a powerhouse.

Farming is hard work and long hours. What's the best part of your day during the growing season?

I love the evenings and those times that technically aren't work hours. I'm out in the fields and it might look like I'm working, but really I'm just interacting with the land, observing it, being among it all. Farming is more of a lifestyle than a job that way. It's just how I want to live: to have the space and time to be with my surroundings and with the natural world.

I also really appreciate all the interactions I have during my workday by living in community. If I was working on a big commercial farm somewhere in rural Ontario, I would be working all day and that would be it. I wouldn't have all the wonderful interruptions, like kids running by, retreat groups asking questions or farmies figuring out which cabbages are ready for harvest.

So it's the community life as much as the farming that you enjoy.

It's incredible to see what is possible when you have a group of people working together with a shared intention. We have a real culture of support here—we're not just growing food, we're also helping each other grow. Producing food is also the link that connects us to the greater community. We have this amazing connection to our neighbours through selling our vegetables at the farmstand.

What do you love to grow these days? Are there certain vegetables or varieties you're really enjoying right now?

I love the heirloom tomato varieties, all the different colours and shapes. Some of my favourites are King Umberto, a beautiful little pink cherry tomato, and Yellow Tiger Stripe, a small yellow tomato with green lines on it. For flavour, I love Costoluto Genovese. They don't store long, but they taste good.

I also love growing a variety of dry bean called orca—when you open them up, they're black and white and actually look like little orca whales.

Where do you live on the farm?

I live in a cabin in the garden that used to be the tool shed. Recently, it was renovated into a beautiful tiny home for me to live in. Now I get the pleasure of living in a perfect space and having all the vegetables as my neighbours.

I really appreciate the versatility of beets: they grow almost year-round here and the recipes change seasonally. We often make this recipe in the late spring and early summer when young beets are tender and precious, but it's also terrific in winter when we can go outside and dig the beets out of snowy garden beds. SERVES 4 TO 6

BEET SALAD *with*
feta and candied pecans

Like most of our vegetables—including carrots and potatoes—I usually don't peel my beets. The outer skin contains a lot of valuable minerals and vitamins, and I think leaving the skin on gives a gorgeous rustic look on the plate. Deep winter is one of the few times I might peel some of the rough parts of the skin off the beets with a paring knife.

Dressing Place ingredients in a bowl and whisk to combine. Set aside.

Beets Wash beets well and remove greens. Leaving them whole, cover with cold water and bring to a boil. Cook over medium heat until tender when pierced with a fork. Drain and set aside to cool.

While beets are cooling, prepare the candied pecans. Heat a cast iron pan to medium-high. Add pecans, and cook a few minutes, stirring until fragrant. Add 1 tbsp butter and 1 tbsp maple syrup or brown sugar. Stir to coat pecans, then remove from heat. Using a heatproof spatula or metal spoon, scrape pecans onto a plate to cool.

When beets are cool enough to handle, slice into rounds, wedges or cubes. Pour dressing over and stir gently to combine. Top with crumbled feta cheese and candied pecans.

Dressing

¼ cup balsamic vinegar

¾ cup extra-virgin olive oil

1 tsp maple syrup or honey

Beets

4 lb medium-sized beets

¾ cup feta cheese

1 cup pecans

1 tbsp butter

1 tbsp maple syrup or brown sugar

Squash blossom risotto is an iconic dish on the farm that we start serving with the arrival of the first squash blossoms in late spring. In Italy this dish is served throughout the spring and summer, and for me it represents the time of year when the many shades of green coming in from the garden become harvest baskets bursting with different colours. SERVES 6 TO 8

summer squash blossom RISOTTO

2 tbsp butter

2 tbsp extra-virgin olive oil

1 medium onion or
1 large leek

3 to 4 small zucchini
(about 2 cups)

10 to 15 zucchini blossoms
(about 2 cups)

5 to 6 cups vegetable stock

2 cups arborio rice

1 cup white wine

2 tbsp finely chopped fresh basil

Salt and pepper to taste

Optional finish

2 tbsp extra-virgin olive oil
or 2 tbsp butter

1 cup grated
Parmigiano-Reggiano

If you're growing zucchini at home, you can harvest your own blossoms. The pollinating male flowers keep the plants producing all season, and by only taking the females—the ones at the end of the zucchini, not on a stem—you will ensure that the bees can keep doing their good work and you will have a steady supply of blossoms all season. Added during the last few minutes of cooking, they impart a beautiful golden colour and delicate flavour to this risotto. For dairy-free guests I omit the butter and cheese, finishing it with a quality olive oil and sea salt, with great results.

Heat butter and olive oil in a medium-sized pot. In a separate pot, heat stock on low. Add finely chopped onion and/or leeks to melted butter and olive oil and sauté until tender. Add chopped zucchini, stir and sauté until beginning to colour. Add rice to pan and sauté while stirring for 3 to 4 minutes. Add wine and stir until absorbed. Lower heat to a simmer. Begin adding heated stock, one ladleful at a time, stirring occasionally (wait until most of the liquid is absorbed before adding the next ladleful).

Continue to add stock for about 25 minutes, until rice is getting tender but is still a little bit firm on the inside, then remove from heat. Gently slice zucchini blossoms and basil, then add to risotto along with additional olive oil or butter and Parmigiano-Reggiano cheese. Season with salt and pepper to taste.

Wild salmon are a vital and sacred part of life on the West Coast. This recipe is based on fresh garden ingredients that are partially blended, creating a wonderful, creamy soup that is not as heavy as traditional dairy-based chowders. Pinot noirs pair well with this recipe, such as one from the cooler Dundee Hills in Oregon, or one of the great BC pinots coming out of the Similkameen Valley. SERVES 6 TO 8

west coast wild
SALMON CHOWDER

You can use leftover cooked salmon for this chowder or start with fresh, raw fish. Any type of salmon will do—I most often work with wild sockeye, coho or spring (aka chinook or king) salmon, but pink salmon also works well in this soup. Sometimes it's nice to add a little smoked salmon in there, too.

If starting with raw salmon, place the fillet on a parchment-lined baking sheet and bake in a 400° oven for about 12 to 15 minutes— until cooked through. After salmon has cooled, separate from skin and break into small pieces, removing all bones.

Dice potatoes into 1-inch pieces; chop celery and onion or leeks. Heat olive oil in large soup pot on medium-high heat. Add onion or leek and sauté until translucent. Add salt, thyme and celery, and continue to sauté for 5 minutes.

Add diced potatoes and water. Bring to a boil, then turn down to a simmer for 20 minutes, until potatoes are tender. Partially blend with immersion blender until soup is approximately half-puréed. Add cooked salmon and optional smoked salmon. Simmer another 10 minutes. If starting with raw salmon simmer an additional 10 minutes to ensure fish is cooked thoroughly. Add salt and fresh black pepper to taste. This soup is very nice served for dinner, with a green salad and a baguette.

3 to 4 cups cooked or raw salmon pieces (about 2 lb)

4 tbsp extra-virgin olive oil

2 tbsp salt

2 tbsp fresh or 1 tbsp dried thyme

1 medium onion or 2 leeks

6 to 8 medium potatoes (about 2 lb)

5 stalks celery

4 cups water

1 cup smoked salmon pieces (optional)

This is one of my favourite whole-vegetable, root-to-leaf dishes. The carrots are given a good scrub but left unpeeled, and almost all of the carrot is used. This recipe also utilizes the lush carrot greens, which are good for you as well as delicious. The carrot top pesto is rich in flavour and brings really gorgeous colour to the finished dish. It's a fantastic way to integrate a vitamin-rich part of the vegetable we normally don't use. SERVES 6 TO 8

ROASTED CARROTS
with carrot top pesto

2 lb carrots

2 cups carrot tops

½ cup + up to 6 tbsp extra-virgin olive oil

½ packed cup grated Parmigiano-Reggiano

½ lemon

1 tsp + pinch salt

This recipe roasts the carrots on high heat, so they become sweet and caramelized. Stir them around a few times during cooking, testing them as you go. You don't want them too firm; they should be nice and tender, which usually takes about an hour.

Heat oven to 400°F. Cut carrots in half lengthwise, or leave whole if very small. In a large bowl, toss carrots in 2 tbsp olive oil and a pinch of salt. Spread carrots onto a parchment-lined baking tray, and bake for 25 to 30 minutes, until they begin to turn golden brown.

Finely chop feathery tops of carrots, discarding tougher stems. Place carrot tops, ½ cup olive oil, Parmigiano-Reggiano and 1 tsp salt in bowl of food processor. Process until thoroughly blended but some texture remains. Add additional olive oil to achieve a pesto-like consistency. Salt and pepper to taste.

When carrots are done roasting, transfer to a serving platter and spoon the pesto over them. Serve warm or at room temperature.

I really believe in the healing qualities of good honey, and making flower- or herb-infused honey is a wonderful way of imparting a little magic into it. The idea in this recipe is to just gently heat your good local honey and pour it over freshly harvested rose petals. MAKES 2 CUPS

rose HONEY

Roses aren't widely known as an edible flower, but they are a fragrant and delicious addition to salads and desserts as well as magical recipes like this rose honey. My favourite for this recipe is the hardy rugosa rose, which has a deep and beautiful fragrance.

The essence of rose imparted through the honey has a very loving energy, and this is one of those recipes where food and medicine cross. When my children are sick I often give them a teaspoon of rose honey; it not only soothes a sore throat but also the heart. This honey is wonderful spread with butter on a freshly baked scone, on hot cereal in the winter, or added to a cup of tea.

Place rose petals in a clean, heatproof glass bowl, and gently heat honey over medium-low heat. You don't want the honey to boil!

When honey is quite liquid and fragrant, remove from heat and pour the warm honey over the petals.

Let sit at room temperature for 3 to 5 days. I leave the bowl on the counter covered with a tea towel. You can taste the honey during this process; it will become more flavourful the longer it sits, so when you are happy with the flavour, simply gently reheat the honey as before, then pour through a colander to strain the rose petals. You can set the petals aside at this point to add to a cake, cookies or other dessert. Pour the honey into a clean glass jar for storing.

2 cups honey

2 cups fresh rose petals

These shortcakes, overflowing with sweet, freshly picked strawberries, are always a highlight of our strawberry season. I love the individual biscuit style of shortcakes in this recipe; they're easy to make and special to serve. For best flavour try to use local, organic strawberries. Fresh blueberries, raspberries and blackberries (or a combination) also all work well for this recipe. MAKES 12 INDIVIDUAL SHORTCAKES

strawberry SHORTCAKE

Shortcake biscuits

2 cups unbleached white flour

2½ tbsp baking powder

1 tbsp sugar + 2 tbsp
for sprinkling on top

½ tsp sea salt

6 tbsp very cold butter

¾ cup milk

Berries and cream

3 cups ripe berries

½ cup sugar

1 cup heavy cream

½ tsp vanilla

1 tsp sugar

Shortcake biscuits Heat oven to 425°F. Cut butter into small pieces and place in a food processor with all shortcake ingredients; pulse until butter is the size of small peas. If there are a few slightly larger or smaller pieces, this will help the shortcakes to become flakey. Transfer to a bowl, make a well in the centre, and stir in milk with a fork, combining until the dough holds together. Do not overmix as this will toughen the biscuits.

Using a tablespoon, divide dough into 12 equal mounds on an ungreased baking tray. Sprinkle a little sugar on top of each one and place in hot oven. Bake on top rack in oven for approximately 12 minutes or until golden on top and bottom. Remove biscuits from baking tray and place on cooling rack.

Berries and cream Remove hulls from strawberries and slice. Place in bowl with ½ cup sugar, gently stir and let sit for at least a few minutes, or up to 1 hour, to allow the berries to release their juices.

Whip heavy cream until soft peaks form, then gently fold in vanilla and 1 tsp sugar. Cut cooled shortcakes in half, top with sliced strawberries (or other berries) and a dollop of whipped cream, then gently place top half of shortcake on top. Serve and enjoy!

"I love the biscuit style of shortcakes in this recipe; they're easy to make and special to serve. For best flavour try to use local, organic berries."

HAIDEE

Cut shortcakes in half, top with sliced berries and a dollop of whipped cream, then add the top half of the shortcake.

HIGH SUMMER

HIGH SUMMER IS A TIME OF YEAR HERE when the light only goes out after 10 p.m. and it reappears before 4 a.m. Sometimes on clear nights it feels as if it stays light all night long. It is a living outside time: lake swimming, bicycle riding, sharing dinners outdoors, sleeping under the moonlight and grazing on new carrots, spinach and the first berries in the fields. We celebrate the long evening hours as we wander the farm. Lots of the farmies go barefoot, the land entering our bodies through our feet, and we relish the connection with the Earth.

Walking by the perennial gardens, there are gentle, exotic whiffs of vanilla in the air wafting from the clerodendrum shrubs. Good old reliable Persicaria amplexicaulis—also known as mountain fleece or firetail—makes big clumps, and bees flock to it in great numbers.

It feels as if the grass grows a foot a week, and in the gardens there is nothing but harvesting and weeding, weeding, weeding—along with mowing, mowing, mowing. This leads us to the perennial activity of haying, all of us working up a spectacular mess of dust as we bring it into the barn.

It's an interesting case of push and pull as summer solstice arrives and we begin the long, slow downward cycle to the end of it all again. Body and soul are now beginning to yearn for some rest after the green man's mad rush toward the light.

The children play high in the trees until late in the day. I find little ones on the path to the strawberries, as they venture out there by themselves to savour the fruit of the season. We are all held in this green bowl of light that seems to reach into forever.

LISA

120

FARMING *practices*

THERE ARE SEVERAL classic organic farming practices we use throughout our operation that are easy to incorporate into any garden. These include certain weeding techniques, mulching, cover cropping, composting and rotating crops.

Weed Control

Weeds are a constant reality of organic farming, and we have several strategies for dealing with them. The first defence is to stop them from germinating at all, by using landscape cloth or other mulch that blocks the sun from the soil. But there are a number of crops that can't be managed well with a ground cover, such as carrots and salad greens, so we are still left with a good amount of weeding to do.

The most efficient manual way to get rid of weeds is with a hoe. While there is a certain beauty to a messy garden, over the years we've found that we enjoy cultivating with slightly more order: straight lines, and planting with even spacing. Gardens like this are a pleasure to hoe. We don't have to be worried about nipping the crop accidentally, as each plant is predictably where it should be.

The secret of hoeing is that in order to get the greatest benefit with the least amount of labour, you should be hoeing before it even looks like you need to. This can be as soon as one week after planting. Hoeing a bed that doesn't even look weedy yet can seem ridiculous, especially with so many other urgent and important things to do around your farm or garden. But even if you can't see them, the weeds are there—they are just very tiny. Do it then and the hoeing is easy, and the weeds vanish before they really take hold. Of course, inevitably some weeds get away from us and we have to pull those by hand.

Mulching

Mulching is the best way to suppress weeds while keeping the soil moisture much more consistent. It's useful for crops that are in the ground all season, such as summer and winter squash. There are two types of mulch: organic and synthetic. For organics, we use mulch hay, which is grass that hasn't gone to seed. If you mulch with hay, be sure to use this rather than regular hay, so it won't seed weeds into your garden.

The benefit to an organic mulch like this is that it will break down over time and become part of the soil. In terms of synthetics, recently we've started using more landscape cloth, which comes in a roll and can be cut to fit an entire garden or garden bed. It's a very neat and effective product that can be used for many years. (Be sure to burn the edges of your landscape cloth, including the planting holes, or it will fray and eventually come apart!)

FACING: Crimson clover in flower—seeded as a cover crop; it's a nitrogen fixer and beneficial to bees and other insects.

Cover Crops

Cover crops, sometimes called green manure crops, hold the ground over winter and replenish the soil when turned under in the spring. These are particularly important in our climate because we get so much rain, which leaches the soil of nutrients. Various types of cover crops benefit the soil by fixing nitrogen, or by absorbing other nutrients that can be turned in, or both. We mainly use winter rye, clover and vetch. For cover crops to work, they need to be well established before winter—so seeding them early enough is key.

The challenge is that we often still have food crops growing in the areas that we want to plant with cover crops. It's time to cut the cover crops down and turn them in when the plants are at their maximum for bulk but before they have gone to seed. This will ensure you are getting the most benefit from your green manure. During the growing season, if we have any time between plantings, we seed buckwheat, which is quick to grow and gives us lots of mass to put back into the ground even after just a few weeks.

Crop Rotation

Crop rotation means growing different crops in succession to benefit the soil, manage pests and assist with weed control. There is a certain amount of flexibility in crop rotation, along with some hard and fast rules. Some of the rotation rules that we live by are: never plant a legume after an allium, alway follow brassicas with potatoes, and mix up the order of shallow- and deep-rooted plants. There are a multitude of other guidelines and rules, too many to list here, so look for one of the guides that illustrate how to effectively rotate three or four different plant types.

Compost

With the type of intensive market gardening that we do, planting and re-planting the same areas throughout the season, we need to constantly replenish the gardens as we go or we run the risk of depleting the soil. Adding sufficient organic compost is essential to maintaining soil health. We make our own compost from all kinds of organic material—weeds that haven't gone to seed, grass clippings, plant stalks and kitchen trimmings—and we also purchase from off-farm to supplement our supply. I think most people would be surprised at how much compost we use to keep the soil fertile and alive. We use about one-half to one inch every time we turn over a crop, which is several times a year.

LIZ

HAYING

THIS IS A huge event on the farm for everyone. We spend days wondering if it is the right time, checking the weather forecasts for possible dates, getting the haying machinery ready and sweeping and organizing the barn ahead of the coming bales.

Then the big event arrives in July, on a day when we think we will have three to five days of sun ahead of us. All the fields get cut with a mower on our tractor, then the next day we bring out the tedder to fluff them up and help them dry. Then out comes the baler! All of the children come out to sit on the wagon when we drive it into the field, following the baler as it chugs along spitting out the new bales.

This is a time of year when the days are long and the sun is high and intense. Everyone gets scratchy and hot and tired as the bales fill up our barn for the winter. This always leads to the need for a swim, and down we all go for a jump into the lake, with bicycles everywhere and clothes thrown willy-nilly on the shore.

It's hard work, but it's a timeless sort of event that happens only once a year here on the farm, and it creates a real bond between everyone who takes part. Often, visitors who take part in this event will say it was one of the best experiences of their lives. I guess the oldtimers had it right—work hard, eat lots and be together!

In past years, some of our mulch hay would be put in the middle of the field to be used relatively soon in the gardens, and some of the children would turn it into an enormous hay fort with many tunnels and openings. We would always know where to find them by the screeches of fun and joy.

After the hay is in, we often gather for a dinner and some time to celebrate. By this time, it's usually dusk, and the fading summer light is so gorgeous that it fills us all with the beauty of the world. All of us recognize the enormous effort that it takes to bring in all that hay, and perhaps that is what makes it such a wonder.

LISA

"It's hard work, but it's a timeless sort of event that happens only once a year here on the farm, and it creates a real bond between everyone who takes part."

LISA

I have been a friend of Lisa's since the days when dances and weddings were hosted in the old barn. The kids, playing in the loft, would be jumping off the hay bales and swinging over the heads of their dancing parents. It has been awesome to witness the gradual evolution of this place from the time when Lisa was labouring to keep her farm afloat to what it has become today.

For the past few years, I have been coming to farm Thursdays as well as taking part in many of the rituals and celebrations. There is something about weeding potatoes, pulling broom or sorting seeds together that elicits authentic rather than surface conversation. In a culture that is typically stratified into generational divides, I find it deeply satisfying to have developed meaningful friendships with people half my age, and younger! Working on the land through the seasons each week has helped me establish a different relationship to time—I'm less driven by preconceived agendas and more in rhythm with the natural flow of my own life.

HONOR (left side of table, fourth from top)

We live up the road from the farm. When my daughter, Lulu, was seven, I just couldn't see us being in the city any longer, although I'd lived in the city all my life. I felt like I owed it to her to bring her to be part of this: living in rhythm with nature and the seasons, which we were missing, and the sense of the community, where it feels like a big family. It's a place where everybody has a purpose, a sense of belonging, and sharing traditions, and joy and grief. It is more like, perhaps, the traditional way—the way of a tribe.

LENKA (third from right)

PLANTING FOR WINTER HARVEST

I LOVE BEING ABLE to walk out to the garden in the middle of winter and dig up beets, carrots and other fresh vegetables. In our climate we're lucky to be able to "store" certain crops out in the field, and they keep us fed through to early spring. Carrots and beets, along with kale, are three of our cold-weather staples.

One of the challenging parts of growing winter vegetables is that you need to seed most of them by early July, just when you're at the peak of harvesting, watering and weeding. It feels counter-intuitive in high summer to be thinking about the carrots that you'll be harvesting in December, but the plants need to be at full size by autumn or your harvest won't be worth the effort.

One of the things that makes it easier to succeed is having a plan already in place. Winter crops need to be part of the whole garden planning that happens near the end of the year.

In our planning we figure out where everything is going to go and how much space we need. Beets and carrots that overwinter in the ground need an area that is well drained, so they don't rot. Kale and other winter greens need to be planted in abundance, because the plants stop growing as the light decreases. Always plant more than you think you'll need for a decent harvest. Proximity is also a factor in our planning. We've noticed that we don't always want to walk clear across the farm to harvest dinner when it's dark and cold, so we try to keep the winter plantings close to home.

LIZ

BUILDING *a culture of trust*

OSTERING A TRUSTING community takes time and effort. Without trust, communication breaks down, walls get put up and resentments creep in. But a culture of trust doesn't just happen magically, and it doesn't happen all at once. It has taken us a long time to build it on the farm—years and years, in fact. It's come gradually through shared experiences, conversations, celebrations and commitments.

Much of this is intentional, through routines and structures we've cultivated, but simply running into people throughout the week has a surprising impact. It keeps us in touch and connected. We bump into each other during the ups and downs of daily life, while we're walking to the farmstand or passing through the courtyard. Important conversations and decisions can happen in unusual places: while stacking wood, through the window of a car stopped on the road, at the compost pile. Just as often these are short five-minute stops or walk-and-chats that in their small way remind us of our common goal of living the best we can together on this farm.

Here are some of the more structured ways that over time have helped us create a culture of trust.

Thursdays: We meet every Thursday to share time, gratitude and work—and eat lunch together as a group. "Thursdays" are a weekly ritual that is the backbone of our community. Everyone shows up. If anyone's missing, we know it's for a good reason.

Weekly Meeting: Working together on the business of running a farm and retreat centre is also a huge element of our community interrelationships. Every Monday morning we meet in the office with those in charge of different areas of farm operation. We deal with any current issues, and make sure we're all aligned in our mission and focus. As with Thursdays, the consistency of these meetings helps reinforce trust, and cultivates the potential of everyone in the community. Things are very dynamic on the farm and always evolving, and we try to continually assess whether everyone is in their best role and getting the support they need.

Off-Sites: Those of us who have lived here for over fifteen years also go off-site for a week once a year, and do a deep dive to talk about whatever is happening on the farm. Drawing from his experience at Guayakí, David urged the core group of us to do this, and has led us through these intensive and fruitful gatherings on an annual basis. The children come with us and it's also a time for them to bond as farm kids, and see us focused as a group on the well-being and direction of the farm. Having the space to delve into bigger issues gives us an essential foundation from which to make decisions in the year to come. We always emerge from these off-sites aligned and reconnected. We've been surprised by how significant these times are.

Many of us also go away as a group to help with my dad's garlic planting in October. We load up a

few cars with camping gear and take a five-hour road trip to his farm in Keremeos, BC. This has become an annual trip. My dad is now in his seventies, and he loves and appreciates the massive work party that arrives on his otherwise quiet property for a few days. It's a fun bonding adventure that builds our relationships in a new place. I think the fact that we choose to go away together is incredible—it must be that we appreciate each other enough to spend more time together. You have to like each other to live in community! This trip also allows us to get out of the usual roles that we play on the farm. We hike, swim in the Similkameen River, do sit spots (see page 176) and spend our evenings around a campfire.

Shared Celebrations: Most of the farm employees live here, so there is inevitable overlap of work and life. We share time together through seasonal celebrations, birthdays and our annual Farmie Crawl, which is our in-house carnival, complete with Stowel Lake Farm—themed costumes. (This year, costumes included our John Deere tractor, our farmstand and a rabbit.) We're a pretty work-focused group most of the time, and the Farmie Crawl in particular is a chance for us to let loose and have fun partying together.

JEN

SUMMER SOLSTICE

Summer solstice comes in the third week of June and it's the longest day of the year. There's so much light—the world feels wide open, and it seems like the days will never end. There are a few times throughout the year that our community gets together to have fun, and this is one of them. On the night of the solstice, or close to that date, we camp out in the lake field, play games, have a fire, tell stories and (of course) share food. We might only be a five-minute walk away from home, but it feels like another world.

Some years we do potato sack, wheelbarrow and three-legged races, and other years we change it up with new games. The afternoon and evening are all about fun, eating, laughing and celebrating these endless summer days with each other and the land.

JEN

FREE RANGE *kids*

OR THE FOUR families raising kids here, it's an incredible experience we're all grateful for—though sometimes it's hard to step back and see it, because we've never known anything else. Having children is a humbling experience, and I would never want to say that raising them on a farm is the best way to do it. But it does seem to have certain advantages.

All of us farm parents are aware of what a privilege it is to have our children experience nature by simply being surrounded by it. The kids have developed their own impressions and had their own adventures on the land without being packed up and taken to a park, or on a camping trip. (Though we do that a lot, too.) Collectively their young minds are tracking and watching all the changes that happen here through the seasons. Some know which apple tree ripens first. Others know which carrots are being harvested, or where the best cedar tree is for climbing. Many of them have a sixth sense for knowing the exact day when the lake is warm enough to swim in.

The children have an almost tribal relationship with each other. They're farm siblings; maybe not quite as close as sisters and brothers, but nearly so. The other adults who live and work on the farm are like one big extended family for them, and each person offers a different form of mentorship. My kids are now aged eight and ten, and they spend more and more time out on the farm on their own. They might be playing at Liz's place, visiting the bunnies or hanging out in the gardens with Meghan. I tell my kids they don't have to be in our house to feel safe. If they're anywhere on the farm, they're at home.

With so many farm siblings, of course, there are inevitable clashes of wills. They've each had many opportunities to work with conflict resolution. We've encouraged them to sit down and resolve their issues, sometimes in little circles with a couple of adults, and the skills of working through conflict seem to be taking root. They've learned to listen to each other, and to talk to each other, with respect (most of the time).

Raising families in such close quarters hasn't always been easy. There's a tendency in us all to be opinionated, especially when it comes to parenting and all the decisions it requires, from sleep to diapering, discipline to choice of school. Here on the farm—where we see and experience each other's parenting choices perhaps more intensely than most—we haven't always been great at speaking about different parenting choices without judgment. Just like our kids, we have lots to learn. Fortunately we're learning in a community of gracious and kind people, willing to forgive and move on.

My hope is that no matter what choices we make as parents, all of the farm kids are growing up with awareness—of the birds they hear, of seasonal changes, of other peoples' needs, of how to contribute positively to the world. What we do know is that the children here emanate joy, they are interested in the world, and they know how to play. They know where their food comes from and aren't afraid to walk barefoot.

JEN

Q&A: *adam and aneta*

ADAM, ANETA and their daughter Hanna left Nova Scotia with the goal of joining an established farm community somewhere in southern BC. With a vintage 1976 Airstream trailer hitched to their truck (converted to run on recycled vegetable oil) they road-tripped through the US, and ultimately ended up on Salt Spring Island.

In some ways they were already farmies: they'd worked on organic farms in Spain for eighteen months after Hanna was born, and then lived for the next nine years on farms in Nova Scotia, one of which included a retreat centre. They picked BC because they wanted to attend some of Jon Young's Washington-based nature connection workshops—programs that we have hosted here on the farm, coincidentally, and that have been transformative for many people in our community. Now they both help manage our retreats, making the farm a warm and welcoming space for visitors.

It sounds like a lot of doors were opened up for you on your journey to Stowel Lake Farm.
ADAM: Everything just worked out. It was like all the arrows pointed here. We were staying on Orcas Island with a friend and everyone there said to us, "Oh, you have to check out Salt Spring, it's our Canadian sister island." When we started looking at Salt Spring online we saw it had the WOLF program, which is basically a Jon Young course for kids. And it turned out my parents' friends had a cottage here that was available for us to use. It all lined up.

ANETA: The cherry on top was that we are fans of the band Rising Appalachia. On our road trip through the US we'd been trying to see their shows, but kept missing them. They were about a month ahead of us on their tour. Then a few months after we first arrived, they played a concert in the barn about a hundred feet from where we had parked our Airstream.

Talk a bit about the work you both do on the farm.
ANETA: People often travel a long way to get here. They leave friends, family and their pets behind, and when they come they don't know what this place is, who lives here or what this is all about. My role is to make sure that when they walk into their room they feel like, "I want to stay here." I set the rooms up and make sure they're nice and tidy, so they have this welcoming feeling. That's a little bit of a mindfulness practice that I try to bring into my job—to be the little fairy nobody sees, the one that makes sure their space is as comfy and welcoming as possible.

ADAM: One my favourite parts of my role on the farm is actually welcoming people physically, so it's the opposite of that for me. When I welcome them I try to give them my full attention and be there just for them—not to just say hello, check their name off on a piece of paper and then rush off. I ask them how they're doing, listen to their stories and share some of my stories as I take them to their room. Then I'll interact with them over the days that they're here by crossing paths every now and then. I really enjoy sharing that deeper connection with visitors, many of whom are coming here to work on themselves as well, through yoga, meditation and other types of personal development. When I give them my full attention it sets that up for them a little, allowing them to settle and find their own ground.

Living on the farm where you work is a unique situation. What do you like about that kind of lifestyle?

ANETA: From our house in the woods, in the mornings I can walk or bike to work. I love going to work and seeing all the different people. You stop and say hi, and people ask how you're doing—it's not a half-hour interaction, but just a brief check in, or people wave and smile. It's just so lovely, an easy flow and interweaving of life and work. Also, for Hanna, it's so nice to live in a community with other children. That was something we didn't really have on the other farms where we lived. The different ages, people, energy and experiences that she gets here that enrich her life—it's such a gift.

ADAM: What brought me to community living is my desire to live sustainably, and to lessen my impact on the Earth. After working on other organic farms and experiencing that lifestyle I realized that I don't want to do it alone. I don't want to be a single farmer, getting up every day to milk the cows, tend the crops, work all day on my own, and then wake up and do it again as a one-man show. Once you can share that lifestyle with other people, that's when it becomes really rich.

You've both lived and worked on many farms. What's been the most surprising thing for you since moving here?

ANETA: For me it's the generosity. The generosity of sharing the land so others can live on it, and all the other things that are just given to you in a place like this. It comes as part of this caretaker's attitude from Lisa and everyone else. There's this idea of stewardship that kind of binds everybody together.

ADAM: I do some of the welcome talks for the retreats, and people often ask, "Why are you guys all living here together? Who is your guru, what is it that binds you as a group?" I had to think about that, and now I believe it's that we all have a desire to take care of this land. Something that I've been struck by here is that everyone has a deep appreciation and respect for the land that we live on. That leads to taking care of the creatures that are here, and taking care of each other. I see it in how Lisa is with anybody who is visiting on the farm—she's always attentive to them and what they might need. "Do you need an extra blanket? Will you be warm enough tonight?"

This is my absolute favourite way to prepare green beans. We make this salad only during the few months of high summer when both green beans and cherry tomatoes are at their peak coming out of the garden. Roasted green beans are such a treat that it's always a challenge to keep from devouring them before they make it into the salad. This is a wonderful dish to pack up as part of a summer picnic, or to enjoy as leftovers the next day. SERVES 4 TO 6

ROASTED GREEN BEAN
and cherry tomato salad

Heat oven to 425°F. Trim ends off of green beans and cut cherry tomatoes in half. Slice onion in ¼-inch half-moon slices. In a large bowl, toss green beans and red onion with olive oil, salt and pepper. Spread evenly on a large baking tray lined with parchment paper and roast in oven for 15 to 20 minutes, or until beans are tender and some are browning a little. Transfer to serving bowl and toss gently with halved cherry tomatoes, balsamic vinegar and optional feta. Let sit a few minutes for the flavours to blend before serving.

4 lb green beans

1 lb cherry tomatoes

1 red onion

¼ cup extra-virgin olive oil

Sea salt

Black pepper

¼ cup balsamic vinegar

1 cup feta, crumbled (optional)

Fresh wild salmon on the grill is a sign that summer is here on the coast. I most often work with coho and sockeye, although my favourite is spring salmon (also known as chinook or king). Grilling on high heat is fast and really locks in the moisture of the fish, especially if you leave it slightly underdone in the middle. SERVES 6 TO 8

GRILLED WILD SALMON
with fresh herb chimichurri

2-lb wild salmon fillet

Chimichurri sauce

2 cups parsley

3 tbsp fresh oregano
(or 1 tbsp dried)

1 tbsp smoked paprika

1 bunch green onions,
or 5 shallots, or a mix

½ cup extra-virgin olive oil

1 tsp sea salt

2 tbsp red wine vinegar

Fresh black pepper

Chimichurri is a South American sauce of finely chopped herbs—it's usually served with red meat, but its bright flavour is a wonderful complement to grilled fish. This recipe is very flexible with which herbs may be used, and the addition of the paprika gives it a sweet, smoky undertone that is lovely. The salmon can be left in a whole fillet, or pre-cut into individual portions.

Heat oven or BBQ to 425°F. Finely chop parsley and oregano (if fresh), along with shallots or green onions. Combine all chimichurri ingredients in a medium bowl.

Place salmon fillets on a parchment-lined baking pan and place in oven or on BBQ grill for 15 to 20 minutes, or until oils in the salmon are rising to the top and turning white. The fillet should feel tender to the touch when pressed with finger. If it is too firm it is overcooked.

Transfer salmon to serving platter and spoon chimichurri generously onto fish. Can be served warm immediately, and it is also delicious at room temperature the next day.

This dish is inspired by a recipe I found in an old French cookbook. The original version had rice mixed in with the zucchini and breadcrumbs on top. Gradually I started taking out the other ingredients and letting the zucchini really shine on its own. This dish has an elegant, classic French flavour with very simple ingredients, and is great eaten warm or at room temperature. Serve with a nice, crisp, minerally white, like a chablis-style chardonnay or a Cortese di Gavi. SERVES 4 TO 6

ZUCCHINI *gratin*

Heat oven to 375°F, and butter a 9 × 12-inch baking dish. Cut zucchini into ½-inch rounds. Heat olive oil in sauté pan, then add zucchini rounds and sauté for about 10 minutes, until just tender. Add roughly chopped basil, and sauté for 3 more minutes. Spread zucchini into prepared pan. Pour cream over—enough to reach the top of the sliced zucchini—and, if you like, top with optional cheese.

Bake about 45 minutes until golden and bubbly. Great warm or cold!

4 lb zucchini
(about 6 to 8 medium size)

2 tbsp extra-virgin olive oil

1 bunch basil

1 tsp salt

1½ cups heavy cream

1 cup grated Parmigiano-Reggiano (optional)

New potatoes and fennel appear in the farm gardens around the same time, and are a match made in heaven. The fennel gets slightly caramelized and sweet while roasting, and goes beautifully with the golden potatoes. Tossing them with some coarse sea salt and torn mint before serving adds a pop of bright, summery flavour. SERVES 6 TO 8

NEW POTATOES
with fennel and mint

3 lb small new potatoes

2 bulbs fennel

1 bunch fresh mint (about 1 cup)

3 tbsp extra-virgin olive oil

1 tbsp coarse sea salt

This dish is wonderful as part of a summer dinner; try it with Herb-Encrusted Lamb (see page 192) and Heirloom Tomato Salad (page 191). It also makes a great picnic dish, and can be made a day ahead of time and served at room temperature.

Heat oven to 400°F. Cut potatoes in half; you should have about 6 cups. Trim green fronds from the fennel and slice the white bulbs thinly, giving about 4 cups. In a large bowl, toss potatoes and fennel together with olive oil. Tear fresh mint into small pieces and set aside.

Place potatoes and fennel on a large, parchment-lined baking tray and roast in oven for 30 to 45 minutes, until golden and tender. Transfer to large serving bowl and combine with mint and coarse salt. Great served warm or cold.

Summer fruit galette is one of my favourite desserts to make: it's a rustic, peasant-style French pastry that is always beautiful and delicious. This recipe is flexible, as you can use almost any fruit that is in season: plums, figs, rhubarb or any kind of berry (fresh or frozen). You just roll the pastry out, spread your layer of ground almonds, add the fresh fruit and fold it over. One of the great tricks of this recipe is that the ground almonds and sugar soak up the juices from the fruit and leave you with luscious, crispy pastry underneath. SERVES 6 TO 8

summer fruit GALETTE

Galette pastry

1⅔ cup flour

1 tsp salt

2 tsp sugar

10 tbsp cold butter

4 to 6 tbsp cold water

Nut filling

1 cup finely ground almonds or walnuts

3 tbsp flour

½ cup sugar

Fruit

1½ lb seasonal fruit (about 4 cups)

1 tbsp sugar, for sprinkling

Cherry tomato variation

1 batch galette pastry (as for fruit galette)

1½ lb cherry tomatoes, cut in half

1 cup ricotta, chèvre or mascarpone cheese

Sea salt, for finishing

Pastry Heat oven to 400°F. To make the pastry, combine flour, sugar and salt in food processor. Cut butter into ¼-inch chunks and add, pulsing until pieces are about the size of a pea. Add cold water just a little at a time and pulse briefly until dough is just holding together. Start with 4 tbsp of water, and add more if needed.

Turn pastry dough out onto your lightly floured counter. Flatten into a round disk, then, using a rolling pin, roll out into a circle approximately 12 inches in diameter. Transfer carefully to a parchment-lined baking tray.

Nut filling Combine all nut filling ingredients and spread mixture in a circle in the middle of pastry, leaving the outer 2 inches of pastry bare. This is the part that will be folded over the fruit.

Fruit Arrange fruit over nut filling. Fold outer 2 inches of pastry over fruit. There should be some fruit in the centre still showing, with loose folds of pastry covering the rest. Sprinkle sugar over the pastry border.

Bake in hot oven for approximately 1 hour, until fruit is bubbling and pastry is golden brown. Let cool completely on baking tray before slicing and serving.

Cherry tomato variation Make pastry and transfer onto baking tray as described above. Spread 1 cup ricotta or chèvre in a circle on the pastry, leaving a 2-inch border for folding over. Arrange cherry tomato halves, cut side down, on top of the cheese. Sprinkle sea salt onto tomatoes. Bake approximately 1 hour, until tomatoes are bubbling and pastry is golden brown.

"This is a simple recipe that allows heirloom tomatoes—with their sweetness and texture— to really shine."

HAIDEE

The Cherry Tomato Variation Spread 1 cup ricotta or chèvre on the pastry, leaving a 2-inch border for folding over. Arrange cherry tomato halves, cut side down, on top of the cheese.

LATE SUMMER

IN LATE SUMMER, WATER RULES OUR DAYS.

Irrigation and watering become very important as we try to ensure all the newly planted crops poke through the crusted soil and up into the light. It's time to check on all the flowers we planted with such fervour in late spring. We don't want to lose them now to the sun, which is hot and demanding. But our long working days are followed with the thrill of so many daylight hours yet available for outside pleasures of all kinds—the promise of our own water time especially, with lake swimming, kayaking and trailing our feet in the sea on beach walks.

The gardens are a riot of rich colours. Asters, rudbeckia, echinacea and many annuals are in their glory. The buddleias stop us with their strong raspberry flavour in the air. Close to the house a stand of sheltered common myrtle invites us in with its scent reminiscent of eucalyptus. Now the sun is lower in the sky, and late in the day everything basks in its warm glow. It's quite extraordinary how the angled slant of the light changes it into something so precious.

The perennial garden becomes a sanctuary, a hideout from the dryness that permeates every cell. The water running there supports the growing life of frogs, salamanders, birds and other creatures. One year, a muskrat spent the whole summer in our small lower pond. The sight of these creatures can be a bit surprising, so it's lucky that not too many of our retreat visitors encountered him!

Down at the lake the same thing happens, as life is attracted to the water. It is wonderful in early evening to watch the young swallows chattering endlessly among the willow branches while their parents hunt for food in the sky or skim along the water.

One morning, early in the middle of August usually, I wake up and sense a change in the air. It's almost imperceptible, but telling for those of us who live and work on the land. There is an excitement in this shift after the long hot days, tinged with the poignancy of leaving summer behind. Our attention on the farm starts to move toward preserving, gathering and stocking up for the winter. The days become a mix of blackberry picking and other preparatory activities, while spending our afternoons and evenings enjoying the last of summer's magic.

LISA

162

TOOLS *we love*

WE LOVE OUR tools. As a small-scale organic farm, some tools work better for us than others. There are new ones out there, along with tried-and-true ones that never get old. (If you are a backyard gardener, some of these may not apply.) Here is an overview of our favourites.

Japanese Hori Hori Knife This small hand tool is so helpful when weeding difficult weeds such as buttercup, yellow dock or perennial thistles. There are many kinds on the market now, so be sure to purchase a high-quality one.

Small Knife Increasingly, we harvest with these little knives. They are inexpensive, versatile and useful. You can find these with knife holders that go on your belt.

Secateurs Otherwise known as pruning shears or clippers, these are simply an extension to any farmer's hand. We use them mostly for harvesting, pruning or opening bales of hay. Some have a wire-cutting option in the blade, which can come in handy.

Hoes Our two favourite types are the collinear hoe and the stirrup hoe. In market gardens, hoes are meant to be used early and often, which can save hours of hand weeding! Don't forget to sharpen them.

D-Handled Fork This tool is useful for digging small patches of grass. Also great for lifting, turning and moving light materials like mulch.

Shovels We have many shovels around that come in lots of shape and sizes. Our favourites are a regular digging shovel with a pointed end, and a square-ended shovel—the latter is perfect for unloading trailers of gravel, soil or compost.

Floating Row Cover Like most organic farms, we have many flying pests. This row cover might not be attractive, but makes it possible to grow carrots without rust fly damage, or cabbages without cabbage moth damage. It's a life-changer. It must be completely pinned down (no holes anywhere) to be effective.

Broadfork You don't want to mix your topsoil, which has lots of organic material in it, with the heavy, sometimes sandy or clay-rich subsoil. We aim to only till the top few inches in preparation for planting, and this tool allows us to loosen the sub-soil without bringing in a big tractor.

Two-Wheeled Tractor Recently we have switched from using our John Deere tractor to a small "walking tractor" in the garden. This tool is an appropriate size for small-scale farming. It has a power take-off system, so it's able to take many different attachments. The flail mower for mowing down old crops and the power harrow that we use for bed preparation are two that we've come to love.

JEN

Vermont Cart This is simply a huge wheelbarrow. It took us many years to finally get one and now we can't imagine not having it. If it gets too heavy, it's easy and fun to pull with two people.

garden PESTS

FARMERS SPEND A lot of time dealing with pests. They're a natural part of the environment, and as an organic farm we try to work with our local ecology and not kill them unless we have to—which sometimes we do. Usually we do it by hand when we catch them chewing on our plants. Wire worms, for example, love to dig into the base of new lettuce plants and eat them from the bottom up. When one of your newly planted lettuces starts to wilt, and all the other ones in the bed are looking good, you know a wire worm is at work. If you dig up the whole plant, find the culprit, squish it between your fingers (gloves optional) and replant the lettuce, often the lettuce will keep on growing.

A couple of other common pests we deal with, such as cabbage moths and carrot rust flies, are managed with a barrier called a floating row cover. No one gets hurt and the vegetables grow protected and happy underneath. Floating row cover only works if it is completely pinned down. You can use planks of wood to hold down the edges (we have also dug one edge in and buried it in dirt to make sure it doesn't come up). One side needs to be accessible so that you can get under the cover to weed or thin your crops. If you look out on your crops and you see your floating row cover flapping in the breeze, you know it's not doing its job!

Organic farming at its best looks at the big picture and asks the right questions. A few years ago we had an infestation of pill bugs in one of our greenhouses, and in early spring they ate every new shoot that emerged from the ground. This had a drastic impact on our first crops of spinach, salad and carrots. We had to ask ourselves why the population of pill bugs—which hadn't been a problem in years past—had exploded.

That particular greenhouse is sited on an outcrop of stone, and at the time the garden soil was contained within a massive thirty-by-forty-five-foot wooden box that sat atop the rock. What we discovered was that the wood from which we'd built the box, now quite old, had become a home for a huge population of pill bugs. The only way we were going to get rid of the pest problem was to get rid of the wood. It took a little bit of time for us to swallow that information, as it meant tearing out the entire box and building something that pill bugs wouldn't like. We ended up using sheets of metal roofing and metal posts to create the box, and we haven't had a problem since.

LIZ

LEFT: Carrots damaged by the Carrot Rust Fly larva.
FACING: Meghan removing floating row cover prior to harvest.

byron's BULL

BACK IN THE eighties, when Salt Spring Island was sleepier, my neighbour Mike Byron had a black bull, which he moved around to service cows in the area. When he was nearby and one of our cows was in heat, that bull wouldn't let anything get in his way.

I was really unaware of the strength of such a big animal. Once, as the bull came strolling by our barn, I thought I'd just put him in a stall so that Mike could come and pick him up. He was very amenable, so I shut him in and went down to the house to call Mike. As I was on the phone, I heard a huge crash and looked out the window to see the bull coming right through the side of the barn!

Mike arrived soon after. He wasn't a big man, but he was always very direct with his actions. He found the bull outside the barn, tied a rope to the ring in the bull's nose, then tied the rope to his pick-up truck. They went slowly up the road to home. He was so low-key through the whole thing I couldn't help but be impressed.

A second adventure for the bull was when he fell in the lake. I happened to be out walking around early one morning, and spied him struggling in the mud, with the water up to his shoulder. Again I called Mike. He came over and we figured the only thing to do was haul him out with our tractor. This took some doing: getting a rope around his neck to begin with, and then trying to haul him upward out of the muck using the bucket of the tractor. Buckets are very useful!

To see this enormous creature dangling from the back of the machine was quite incredible—and dangerous for him—but it was over in an instant. As soon as he was out he ambled off to graze in the field as if nothing had happened at all. Just another day on the farm.

We had many encounters with animals from the Byron farm. On full-moon nights, his horses liked to come running down Reynolds Road and right up to our barn to visit the horses we had inside in our stalls. This would cause the most enormous excitement and it would usually take us an hour or more in the middle of the night to get them to run away home.

Those nights with the neighbour's animals weren't the only excitement the horses on our farm have had. One night, one of our little ponies, Taco, managed to get himself out of his stall. He was very talented with his mouth and had twisted open the latch. After that, he proceeded to open all the other stalls. By the time I realized that something was amiss, every horse we boarded was out running around—eating, neighing and relishing their freedom. Taco, the little pony, was just standing happily in the middle of the barn as if to say, "Look how clever I am."

LISA

community AND CONFLICT

Living in community can be challenging. Inevitably, conflicts arise, and when they do we try our best to respond to them in a way that is kind, compassionate and also realistic for the needs of the farm and those who live here. One of the best ways we've found to increase harmony and minimize conflict is by making sure that the group of us who have lived on the farm the longest are clear about, and aligned with, its mission and direction. This happens in an ongoing way, through conversations and our Thursday gatherings. It's also greatly helped by quarterly meetings and our annual off-site retreats.

By living in community we acknowledge that we are welcoming in some conflict. What we strive for in it all is balance. We always have to be willing to question if it is still working, still worth all the effort and time we put in. If it's not, something needs to change. There will of course be difficulties living closely with other people, but the benefits need to outweigh the challenges.

Like any organization, we deal with small conflicts and issues that come up daily or weekly. When these day-to-day issues arise, we try to handle them in a thoughtful way, making sure people feel heard and understood—and that we're seeing the big picture so that we can respond appropriately. We had a situation recently where one of our community members damaged a farm-owned vehicle. She came to us very sorry and apologetic. We discussed her paying for the repair, but she felt so badly that she was going to stop using the car. We didn't want her to do that. We wanted her to practice driving! "Take the car out. Go by yourself. Go regularly. Learn how this car works. This is a tool for you now and a skill that you can use for the rest of your life." We encouraged her to use the car more.

Continual communication—along with opportunities to step back and renew our understanding of what we're all doing together—is essential to having everything run well. But even with all of that, things still come up. The biggest and most difficult issues often arise when someone is not in the right role on the farm, or is not a good fit for the community. In these cases, not everyone always agrees, and we have had to make some tough decisions in order to put the farm first.

For the farm to thrive, everyone needs to feel that they can thrive here as an individual. Being in the right role is essential to feeling like a connected and contributing member of the community. We've found that it is so important to really see each other, so that we can recognize each person's gifts. Everyone's way of contributing is so individual.

A few years ago, one of our core families was considering leaving because they weren't sure if being here was a good fit for them. They'd been

here over a decade and many of us were not only sad at the thought of them leaving, but also afraid the whole community would fall apart if they did. It was a challenging time for all of us. Over a few months, we held several special meetings to talk through all of our feelings and concerns, though we all knew they ultimately had a private decision to make and that we had to trust the process. In the end, they decided to stay.

While the situation was tough to deal with, it reinforced what we've learned about the value of patience and "being with" a situation. The temptation when things get uncomfortable is to relieve the tension by either forcing a decision too soon or sweeping things under the rug. If you don't do either of those things, you just have to allow things to be as they are, and trust that the best outcome for everyone will arise if given space and time. As in all relationships, big issues resurface and may be dealt with over and over again, even if you think you're done!

LIZ

We grow the bulk of our tomatoes in our greenhouses. This allows valuable season extension, particularly in the fall when tomatoes are susceptible to the fungal disease called blight. In the varieties we grow we mainly look for taste, but shelf life, versatility and yield are important too. Each year we taste the tomatoes to determine the ones we like best. Brandywine, Costoluto Genovese, King Umberto and Black Prince are some of our favourite heirloom plants from which we have been saving seed for a few decades, but we're always making room for new varieties.

SIT SPOTS

SIT SPOTS ARE a straightforward but powerful awareness and centring practice: you simply sit outside and observe. The idea is to be in all of your senses and see what happens. It's an easy way to awaken curiosity about, and engagement with, the natural world that surrounds us.

Several of us on the farm learned it through our kids, who attend (or have attended) a nature connection and mentoring program on the island, based on the 8 Shields model developed by Jon Young. A core part of sit spots is focusing on sensual perception: not only seeing where you are but also listening to the sounds of nature around you, feeling the ground you're sitting on, smelling (and even tasting!) the air as you breathe it in.

Often what I notice first is the smell of the air, and the feeling of it on my skin. Tuning into sound is also a great way to stay in the present moment. Listening to sounds from all directions—the farthest sounds and the ones closer in—brings you back to what's happening right now.

Some of us do sit spots regularly, and others do it from time to time, integrating the principles into their walks or meditations. What really brings it alive is to be able to share with others what you've experienced. We've done this as a group on the farm, both kids and adults, and it is always surprising how meaningful such a simple thing can be. Everyone goes off for a sit spot for fifteen to twenty minutes, one person calls us all back, and then we sit together and talk about what we observed, noticed or had questions about.

It's a good idea to pick a place as close to home as possible. You don't have to seek out a dramatic spot on top of a mountain. I usually sit on a rock that faces into the woods, about four metres from my house; our head farmer, Meghan, likes to sit on a dock on the pond behind her house. If you're in the city, try to find somewhere that lets you directly experience the sky, woods and earth. It could be as simple as your backyard or front porch. The practice deepens if you return to the same spot each time—your observations expand and your relationship with that place gets more profound.

LIZ

Q&A: *josh*

JOSH GREW UP on South Salt Spring Island. His father was dear friends with Lisa, and Josh shared many celebrations while growing up with the Lloyd family on the farm, from birthdays to barn dances. In his twenties, Josh lived with Haidee in a driftwood cabin in Bamfield, and they later moved onto Mansell Farm on Salt Spring. Their first two sons were born in the farmhouse there, and Josh worked for several years taking care of the land and the forests while developing his woodworking career.

Josh and Haidee moved onto Stowel Lake Farm in 2005, and for many years Josh was in charge of maintaining the farm's infrastructure. Now, he focuses entirely on his passion for woodworking and vehicles. Josh and Haidee have raised their four children here, making the farm their home. Josh and family continue to travel and adventure together, bringing inspiration from out in the larger world back to their rich farm life.

What are your thoughts on living in community here on the farm?

It's a great way to go, to be able to live in a situation where you can communally share things together, like a truck. Not everyone needs their own work truck. You can share it with five other people and you realize, "Wow, this actually works." Here, we also share the sawmill and a workshop, and all of the tractors and farm machines are available. It is incredibly valuable to have things like tools and equipment accessible to us all, and in turn everyone can be more productive through these resources that are shared in a respectful, organized way.

How about the social side?

With a family of six, our home is a pretty lively social hub on the farm. I love welcoming extended family and friends into our home to celebrate, whether it's someone's birthday or just a beautiful summer evening that we can enjoy with great food and drinks. Our home is really welcoming, and the greater farm is like an extension of our home, warm and enriching to everyone who comes to gather here. I have so many incredible memories of the barn dances that Lisa used to hold here in the old days. These days we still love gathering in the barn, creating our own traditions within that beautiful space.

The core crew on the farm is pretty close, like family. We're all quite different and have our different views on how we go about things, which helps to keep life diverse and interesting. There is a common vision and love for one another that keeps us all on track, so any difference of opinion tends to enrich our process rather than undermine it. I think it is really important to live in some kind of multi-generational situation. So many places in the world live that way—where the grandparents are living in the house with the family and the aunt and uncle are in the house next door. It just makes so much sense. I really feel hopeful that our culture

179

will embrace this way of life more in the future, as it can be so deeply rewarding and is also highly practical when raising families.

Talk about your passion for woodworking.

My dad was a prolific woodworker. He was a real West Coast artist, and he left a legacy of beautiful wooden sculptures, fences, furniture and signs all around Salt Spring. I grew up in a highly creative environment where creating beauty with wood played a huge role in our home. As a young man I was lucky enough to have my dad as a mentor and I learned how to work with wood, which continues to be the most fulfilling work that I do. I feel like I can express myself creatively when I'm sculpting wood. I have the same style as my dad, rounding and softening the edges and working with the organic nature of the wood, enhancing the beauty that is already there.

And now you're bringing that work into customizing vehicles?

I love vehicles of all sorts. I've always done woodwork in and on my campers and vans. When you look at what's out there for vehicles and campers, there's a lot of room to evolve toward a more beautiful, earthy aesthetic. That's the direction my career is taking now, to bring wood into and onto vehicles, customizing them with these curved, soft, warm woods. I'd actually love to build out an electric car, a little two-seater sports car maybe, with a steel frame but otherwise made of wood. That would be awesome.

I've been familiar with Stowel Lake Farm for my whole life, since my parents' cheese company is right across the street. I'd always been drawn to this place. When walking by I'd hear the kids laughing and playing, and it always gave me a sense of wholeness and wholesomeness.

In general, what I'm learning here that is so valuable is a way of life. It's not the specific details of farming, though there are so many and there's so much to learn. My life here is so rich and abundant in the people I'm with, in the food I get to eat, and in my spiritual practice. What I'm doing now—being outdoors, working with the land, being intimate with it—is, for me, far more spiritual than any other practice I've ever done. Overall I think what I'm learning is the answer to the question, "What makes up a life—a really rich, true life?"

THEA (left)

This soup really showcases the flavour of a few simple summer ingredients. Fresh zucchini and basil are sautéed until fragrant, then all you need is water, sea salt and pepper to turn it into a creamy, satisfying soup. When starting with high-quality vegetables I often find that using water instead of stock in soup works very well. The vegetable themselves have so much flavour. SERVES 4 TO 6

ZUCCHINI *basil soup*

In the summer many gardens have an abundance of zucchini, and this simple recipe really lets it shine as the great vegetable it is. Credit for this recipe goes to my sous chef, Amrei, who learned it from her German grandmother.

Trim off ends of zucchini and slice into ¼-inch-thick rounds. Roughly chop basil. Heat olive oil in a large stockpot and add zucchini. Sauté for 10 minutes, until it starts to wilt and get fragrant. Add chopped basil and salt and sauté for another 10 minutes.

Add 6 cups water, bring to a boil, then simmer for 20 minutes. Purée with immersion blender until very smooth—this can also be done in batches, carefully, in a regular blender. Add sea salt and pepper to taste. Can be garnished with a little fresh basil or parsley.

¼ cup extra-virgin olive oil

3 lb zucchini

2 cups fresh basil

4 cups water

1 tsp salt

Salt and fresh ground black pepper to taste

Handful of basil or parsley for garnish (optional)

For many years I preserved our summer tomatoes by making pasta sauce or canning whole tomatoes. These days slow roasting is pretty much the only way that I preserve tomatoes: the slow cooking deepens and preserves that great summer sweetness. Roasting is best done with roma tomatoes because they're really sturdy and not overly juicy, but you can really roast any variety, or a mix of whatever tomatoes you have on hand. MAKES ABOUT 4 CUPS

slow roasted TOMATOES

15 to 20 roma tomatoes (about 3 lb)

½ cup extra-virgin olive oil

2 tsp salt

Fresh or dried thyme

I put these roasted tomatoes into sealable bags and tuck them in the freezer to use all winter. They thaw quickly and are such a great addition to many dishes. They can be served as antipasti on a cheeseboard just as they are, and they're also a brilliant foundation for soups and stews that really want that deep tomato flavour—tortilla soup, chili, minestrone and many others.

Heat oven to 275°F. Cut tomatoes in half and arrange cut side up on a parchment-lined baking tray. Drizzle olive oil over tomatoes, then sprinkle with salt and fresh or dried thyme. Place in oven and roast for 3 hours or so, until looking quite dry but still tender.

This recipe really captures the magical essence of summer. There are many versions of stuffed blossoms that require dipping in batter, but the following sauté method highlights their pure, delicate flavour. SERVES 4

SUMMER SQUASH BLOSSOMS
stuffed with fresh ricotta

Fresh Ricotta

8 cups milk

1 cup heavy cream

1 tsp salt

¼ cup fresh lemon juice

1 package cheesecloth

MAKES 2 CUPS

I love the beauty of brand-new baby summer squash (aka zucchini) and their blossoms—and the pleasure of walking through the patch to gently harvest them, trying to keep the blossoms attached to the squash. I lay them in a basket and bring them into the kitchen, preparing them simply with a little fresh cheese inside the blossoms and a quick sauté in olive oil. If you end up with some blossoms that have separated, just prepare and cook them alongside the other ones.

You can enjoy these hot out of the pan or at room temperature as an appetizer; served on a rustic wooden board or platter they are simply stunning. I like to offer these with a chilled gavi, an exquisite, food-friendly white wine made entirely from Cortese grapes in Italy's Piedmont region. Gavi is traditionally served with vegetable-based starters, and really complements the young zucchini and the creaminess of the fresh, melting cheese.

Fresh ricotta Bring milk and cream just to the boiling point in a large pot. Turn heat to low and simmer for 5 minutes. Add salt and stir to combine. Add lemon juice, stir to combine and remove from heat. You should see the milk begin to curdle immediately. Set aside for 10 minutes.

Line a colander or sieve with 2 layers of cheesecloth and set in mixing bowl, leaving enough room below bottom of colander for the whey (the liquid that separates from the cheese curds) to drip through into the bowl.

Gently pour milk mixture into the lined colander. Let hang for approximately 20 minutes, until most of liquid has dripped through into the bowl and you are left with the soft and creamy ricotta. Transfer to smaller bowl.

Because this recipe makes 2 cups you'll have 1 cup left over after making the summer squash recipe. It's wonderful served straight away—spread on crostini and drizzled with honey as part of a cheeseboard, for instance, or will keep in the fridge for up to a week.

Stuffed squash blossoms Mix chèvre or ricotta with 1 tsp salt in small bowl. Gently spoon 1 tbsp cheese mixture into each zucchini blossom. Twist petals to enclose. Heat olive oil in large sauté pan on medium-high heat. Carefully place each zucchini in pan. Sauté for 3 to 5 minutes, turn, and sauté another 3 to 5 minutes, until zucchini are turning light golden brown.

Carefully transfer to serving platter. If any blossoms come unattached, simply place on the platter beside zucchini. Drizzle with the extra 2 tbsp olive oil, and sprinkle with grated Parmigiano-Reggiano and coarse salt.

Stuffed squash blossoms

1 cup fresh ricotta (or chèvre)

¼ tsp salt

20 baby zucchini,
 with blossoms attached

3 tbsp extra-virgin olive oil

Coarse sea salt

Freshly grated
Parmigiano-Reggiano

2 tbsp extra-virgin olive oil

I wait all year for that glorious summer day when our first tomatoes are ripe. Farm life gets richer and sweeter with tomato sandwiches, cherry tomatoes eaten out of hand, and simple salads like this one. All that you need is some good olive oil, sea salt and a little fresh basil to create this salad of thickly sliced, sun-warmed tomatoes. SERVES 4 TO 6

HEIRLOOM *tomato salad*

A few of my favourite heritage varieties are the Costoluto Genovese, an old Italian variety with deep crevices coming down from the stem; the beautiful Black Krim with its deep purple-brown colour; and a large, luscious variety called Brandywine.

Slice tomatoes in rounds and arrange on a platter, tucking basil leaves in and around tomatoes. Drizzle olive oil and sprinkle salt over tomatoes, and enjoy! Truffle-infused olive oil can be used if you have it.

3 lb ripe summer tomatoes

2 tbsp quality
extra-virgin olive oil

Coarse sea salt

One bunch fresh basil

191

This is a summer favourite on the farm: tender, juicy lamb infused with the flavours of fresh herbs and garlic. Roasting the lamb on the barbecue will impart beautiful chargrilled flavour, but it is also delicious roasted on high heat in the oven. The fresh lavender flowers are optional, but if you have access to fresh or dried lavender I encourage you to try adding it; it gives the roast lamb a lovely herbaceous flavour. SERVES 6 TO 8

herb-encrusted
LEG OF LAMB

1 bone-in leg of lamb (4 to 6 lb)

1 large bunch flat-leaf parsley

1 bunch fresh basil

3 to 5 sprigs fresh rosemary

3 to 5 garlic cloves

2 tbsp freshly ground
black pepper

2 tsp salt

3 to 4 tbsp extra-virgin olive oil

2 tbsp fresh (or 1 tbsp dried)
lavender flowers (optional)

This recipe is best if you can allow the lamb to marinate with the herb mixture for 12 to 24 hours prior to cooking. A good, earthy Bordeaux pairs very well with this recipe, or a full-bodied syrah with notes of black fruit and herbs. If there are any leftovers, they make a fantastic cold lunch the next day—packed between thick slices of country bread, or served alongside a crisp green salad with tomato, feta and olives.

Finely chop all herbs and mince the garlic. Place herbs, garlic, olive oil, salt and pepper into a bowl and combine. Using your hands, rub mixture all over the lamb leg. At this point you can set the lamb back in the fridge to marinate for 12 to 24 hours, or roast right away. If you refrigerate it, take it out of the fridge and allow it to stand for 20 minutes or so before roasting.

When ready to roast the lamb, heat oven or barbecue to 450°F. Place lamb leg into roasting pan and put in hot oven, or directly on grill in hot barbecue. After 10 minutes, turn heat down to 325°F. Allow leg to roast until a thermometer inserted into the thickest part of the meat reads 125 to 135°F for medium rare, or 135 to 145°F for medium (about 1½ to 2 hours). The temperature will continue to rise up to 5° after lamb is removed from heat.

Remove from oven or barbecue, cover loosely with aluminum foil, and let rest for 15 to 20 minutes before carving. Transfer to serving platter and drizzle with the herb-rich pan juices.

During the hot August days when blueberries are coming in from the fields, we make this recipe almost daily in our kitchen. We can't get enough of the warm berries with a touch of lemon in this rich, moist cake. I often serve it warm out of the oven as is, or if there is a birthday it can be topped with whipped cream and fresh berries—or iced with a vanilla buttercream frosting. There are many variations that I incorporate throughout the seasons, substituting fresh cranberries and orange zest in the autumn, diced apple and cinnamon in the winter and chopped fresh rhubarb and pecans in the spring. SERVES 10 TO 12

fresh blueberry LEMON CAKE

Heat oven to 350°F. Lightly oil or butter a 10-inch springform pan or a 9 × 12-inch baking pan. In a large bowl, cream butter and sugar until light and fluffy. (This can be done by hand or with an electric mixer on medium.) Mix in eggs, yogurt, vanilla and lemon zest.

In a separate bowl, combine flour, baking powder, baking soda and sea salt. Add dry ingredients to wet and stir to combine thoroughly. Spread batter in prepared pan, sprinkle blueberries over batter and bake for about 1 hour or until a toothpick comes out clean.

Allow cake to cool completely. Then serve it on its own, or, as an option, top with whipped cream or your favourite frosting.

2 cups fresh or frozen blueberries

1 cup soft butter

1 cup sugar

2 eggs

1 cup yogurt

1 tsp vanilla extract

Zest of 2 lemons

2 cups unbleached white flour (or gluten-free flour)

2 tsp baking powder

½ tsp baking soda

½ tsp sea salt

195

AUTUMN

WITH THE ONSET OF AUTUMN WE anticipate the coming of winter and feel a sense of loss as the wheel turns again toward the dark. However, as farmers in the northern hemisphere, we feel gratitude for this shift. Each season is rich with possibility, and autumn has its particular gifts. One is definitely colour. Fall's palette is a visual feast: green to gold to yellow-pink to russet and deep red. So many indigenous species—maples, willows, cascara and Indian plum—turn gorgeous shades of yellow in the autumn.

While this is happening all around us, as farmers we're busy putting beds to sleep; as permaculturists we're preparing the ground and planting trees and shrubs; as seed-savers we're collecting for the seasons ahead; and as homeowners we're gathering and preserving tomatoes, fruit and other veggies and bringing in the last of the winter wood. We feel like squirrels sometimes. We are very much a part of the Earth's cycles, preparing for the days to come like all creatures do in this corner of the world.

The migratory birds have gone, but our winter residents are busy in the seed-heads of the sown grains and sunflowers, which are everywhere, farm and garden alike. Consequently, we leave most plants standing in the perennial garden and in the permaculture area on the hillside above the Gate-house. It is such a pleasure to watch creatures find their nourishment there in the shortening days. The bees are still busy on warm autumn afternoons but it won't be long before it is pretty quiet, except for the activity of winter birds such as chickadees, wrens, sparrows, juncos and others.

In the garden we take stock of our successes and conditions, and decide to renovate certain areas or add new specimens, or both. I believe in fall planting despite the vagaries of the season, because plants get settled in and then are ready to really grow in the spring. So one of the big gifts of fall for me is the chance to work in this way again,

getting back in the garden from dawn to dusk after the heat of the summer. This time is more like the beginning of our year.

On the permaculture hillside, this is a time of deciding what we can plant now, checking on whether our cuttings are big enough to plant out on the swales, and deciding to put out the little seedlings we have been nurturing for a few years. Every year I dare to experiment more with site location, conditions and how plant guilds work. This year my son Hamish and I planted elderberry, grape and fig cuttings, along with some fruit trees and many small pines that were finally ready to be placed out in the big world. Then we cardboarded and mulched it all for the winter. This is such an exciting project for me, and for us, to be planting a new perennial food garden for the future.

LISA

CHICKENS

W E HAVE HAD chickens on the farm since the beginning of our lives here. Now they live further away from the main hub of the farm, which has its blessings as there is less destruction in the gardens and no more unwanted offerings on doorsteps. The dark side of this is that we don't always catch sight of the hungry hawks—or the ravens, eagles and raccoons—that have them in mind for lunch or dinner.

One year the ravens were actually waltzing right into the chicken house through their morning exit door and taking all the eggs. Every day. Ravens are very clever birds, so we had to find an equally clever strategy for us and our chickens. I did some reading and learned that ravens do not like to feel enclosed. With this in mind, we built a small box inside the entrance to the chicken house—to get in, the ravens had to go in the box and navigate a turn to find a way inside. The chickens didn't mind, but the ravens were having none of it. A simple resolution to a challenging problem.

All in all, as farmers we feel that we've struck a good balance with the natural world. We didn't want to try to rid our landscape of ravens; we admire the raven who can find a way into the henhouse. If any of them decide that fresh eggs outweigh navigating dark corners, we'll have to use our wits again to foil this intelligent bird. Working with natural systems and not against them is one of our goals.

A few years ago, we decided to buy an incubator to try to hatch our own chicks. This is quite a procedure, and we have not yet perfected this method of providing new hens for egg production. We still seem to get a preponderance of roosters, who then race around the chicken yard bothering the hens and fighting with each other until they end up in the stew pot. Raising chickens appears to be like sowing carrots—mundane, not highly regarded as a skill, and yet a huge amount of time is needed to take care of them.

In the meantime, the hens go on doing what they do best: laying eggs, finding new spots to hide in the barn hay, searching all day for tender grubs in the grass and fluffing up their feathers with dust baths. The children love visiting the barnyard and watching the hens' antics and we all appreciate what they bring us in the form of that perfect egg.

LISA

ROCK PICKING

A FEW MONTHS back I had a conversation with a member of the Reynolds family who owned the farm before we bought it. I asked her what she remembered, and one of the memories that came to mind for her was all the rocks she had to pick. What a timeless job it is!

In the late seventies Mum used to have rock-picking parties on the farm: "Come pick some rocks and have a beer at the end." People loved it.

When we harvested the winter squash this year, Meghan suggested we do a quick rock-pick of the field before she planted the cover crop of winter rye and vetch. Walking the field with my bucketful of rocks, I remembered all the times I had rock-picked in my life, back to when I was six years old. It is such a satisfying job. The stones we pull from our soil here are mostly fist-sized, but we have unearthed rocks—some the size of a suitcase—that required a tractor to extract them.

JEN

the FARMSTAND

OVER THE YEARS of cultivating a large market garden we've tried many different ways of getting our produce to customers. For years we attended two farmers markets per week. We also sold to local grocery stores and ran a CSA (Community Supported Agriculture) program that at one point had 60 members. Since 2010 we've had a farmstand, and over the years we've focused on developing a customer base for it. Now it's overtaken all the other, more labour-intensive ways we've tried to sell our produce. All of it is either sold through our farmstand or used in catering our retreats. This is food with zero miles on it. This approach really works beautifully for us and for all of our Salt Spring neighbours who want locally grown vegetables, fruit and flowers.

Josh and his brother-in-law, Luke, used matching curved cedar logs from our forest to build the beautiful farmstand structure now at the entrance to the farm. At first it was too big for our needs, and we weren't exactly sure how much traffic it was going to get. It had just one fridge with a few shelves and a lot of empty space. Now we have three packed fridges, and in the summer we still have to restock them two or three times a day to supply our regular customers.

We put a lot of effort into making the farmstand a welcoming place for visitors, one where they know they can consistently find quality produce, and where they can easily serve themselves. Our goal is to have staple vegetables—salad mix, greens, carrots, kale, cucumbers and tomatoes—always available in season so people can count on getting what they need. In the spring we also sell hundreds of vegetable and annual flower starts, as well as plants from the perennial garden throughout the year.

Today we keep the farmstand open all the time and use the honour system. This has been very successful for us. There's a small loss using this method, but it's not remotely close to the expense of hiring someone to sell the produce. Our farmers can spend more time farming and less time being salespeople.

JEN

AUTUMN *traditions*

SOME OF OUR favourite traditions take place in the fall, when things finally begin to wind down with both our farming operation and our retreats. Near the beginning of November some folks leave the farm for the winter, and before they do it's a perfect opportunity to celebrate the season we've had and all the work we've done: a time to mark the change of seasons, take a break and get a little crazy after a lot of hard work.

The Farmie Crawl is our adult version of Halloween, though it usually happens a week or two before. All of us dress up according to some theme—woodland creatures, or some aspect of life on the farm—and everybody opens up their house for a visit by the travelling party. At each house we eat, drink, dance, sing and generally have a great time being silly. There's something ancient and carnivalesque about traipsing around in the dark in full costume.

A couple of days before Halloween we have a pumpkin-carving party. We gather outside around a bonfire, bring food to share—soup and bread, or roasted pumpkin seeds and popcorn—and carve our jack-o'-lanterns. Compared to winter solstice preparations, which can be pretty involved, we appreciate how simple this one is: all you have to do is show up with a pumpkin and a knife. The best part is lighting them up and seeing what everyone has created.

Another well-loved tradition on the farm is a Halloween character called Screamy. His true identity remains a mystery, but in the days before Halloween, signs appear around the farm in the middle of the night—including on the gate the kids pass through to go to school—announcing his return. On Halloween night, with a soundtrack of spooky music blaring in the background, Screamy takes over Roman's house and lurches around in a black cloak with a terrifying mask. Conversations among the kids about who Screamy really is last all year. Jen's son Rio once proposed inviting Screamy and Roman to his birthday party, so he could determine once and for all if they really were two separate people.

LIZ

LEFT: Roasting the seeds after carving your Halloween pumpkin is simple, fun and tasty, and you can do it over an open fire or on the stovetop. Just give the seeds a bit of a rub with a tea towel to loosen any bits of pumpkin, then either dry roast them or drizzle with a little oil in a cast iron pan. Stir them around until golden brown, sprinkle with sea salt and enjoy!

FACING: In mid-November we have a Lantern Walk. We started this tradition as something to do with the kids as the days grow shorter, and then we fell in love with it. It is so beautiful to walk at night with homemade lanterns glowing in the dark, sometimes singing, sometimes in silence. For us this tradition is about kindling the inner light, the inner fire, as the seasonal darkness around us increases.

THANKSGIVING

THANKSGIVING IS ABOUT gratitude for the life we live, for the clean food and water we have access to, for our families, for each other and beyond. It is also about celebrating our farming season. We make a huge feast using vegetables and meat from the farm and enjoy it together.

Because we do our best to foster a culture of gratitude on the farm, on Thanksgiving we take this practice further with the creation of our Thanksgiving altar.

A few days before the feast, we set up a long table as the altar. We don't decorate ahead of time; instead it becomes this beautiful display from all of the things people place on it. Over the days leading up to Thanksgiving, people gradually fill the table with treasures that represent something they're grateful for and want to hold in that space. This could be pictures of loved ones, river stones, favourite vegetables, a favourite tool or piece of knitting—whatever represents something for which they want to give thanks.

On the day of our Thanksgiving gathering, before or after dinner, we get up one by one to share with the others something about the item we brought. We talk about what we're grateful for in our lives as a whole, with a bit of reflection on the past year. Children and adults all take turns, and this simple ritual makes Thanksgiving a way to feed our souls and spirits, as well as our bodies.

The great thing about this ritual is how easy and accessible it is. One year we had a friend of my dad's at Thanksgiving who was eighty-six years old and had never participated in a sharing circle. Witnessing what he was grateful for in his life in that moment was a deeply moving experience for all of us who were listening. It would bring me great joy to hear that other families and gatherings try this at their Thanksgiving celebrations.

JEN

FACING: India sharing her gratitude at Thanksgiving.

SEED *saving*

JENNIFER AND I got into seed saving early in our farming life, with the encouragement of Dan Jason at Salt Spring Seeds. We had been farming for a year or so with a group of other young people when we agreed to start saving seeds for Dan. We started growing a lot right away—collecting seeds for twenty different varieties of lettuce, multiple types of peas and tomatoes, squash, cucumbers, peppers and more.

I have always loved the process of saving seed. As vegetable farmers we generally harvest the plant before it can fulfill its destiny as a seed producer. It's exciting to let some of the plants go through their full life cycle, and see them transform from seedling to full maturity to seed production and death. Seed saving allows you to really experience how much beauty there is in each stage of development.

We've saved some varieties continuously for almost twenty years. Over this time we've formed a relationship with these cultivars and have found many favourites. One is a fairly rare paste tomato called Maria's that was brought to Canada by a Hungarian family. Another one is a butter lettuce that we call Continuity, also known as "Merveille de Quatre Saisons." Calvert is an edible-pod climbing pea that is giant and delicious. Red Russian kale is a good old standby and an incredible producer throughout the seasons.

Seeds and plants adapt to their environment. As you grow and select for your own purposes you start to create seeds that are well-suited to your region's specific climate, light and soil. This is something that takes many years, but it is one of the benefits of saving your own seeds.

It's important for farmers to get know the seed-savers in their region. Keeping seed in the hands of farmers and the people, not corporations, is vital for keeping control over our food and food production. Being seed savers has made us much more self-sufficient, and has connected us to a lineage of farmers who have done this same process for centuries.

Saving Seed: Lettuce

It's easy and fun to collect lettuce seed, and there are many beautiful heirloom varieties. Lettuce is also self-pollinating, so you don't have to worry about it crossing with anything else. Ideally, leave six to twelve plants from an early spring planting in the ground and let them to go to seed. The lettuce will mature and get overripe, and soon the centre of the lettuce will start to shoot up. It's amazing to see. They get so tall—four to five feet! Flowers will form at the top, and you'll know seeds are forming when the flowers turn into white fluff (similar to dandelions, but smaller).

To check if the seed is ready, pull off a bit of fluff—you will see the seeds underneath. Harvest by leaving the plant in the ground and bending it over a container, such as a bucket or plastic bin (see picture on facing page). Bang the seed heads against the side of the container to dislodge the seeds. By leaving the plants in the ground you can return for another harvest if all of the seeds haven't matured at the same time.

FACING: Leek seeds drying down inside.
RIGHT: Black turtle beans.

Saving Seed: Dill & Cilantro

It's dead simple to save seed from cilantro and dill. They're self-pollinating, so you don't have to worry about them crossing with other plants. Let one of your early plantings bolt, flower and form seeds. It takes a long time—a couple of months—for seeds to develop after they flower, and you want to have enough time in late summer and autumn to let the seeds fully form in the field and dry down.

Seeds are ready when you can see them on the ground, or if they fall off when you touch them. If they haven't had long enough to dry where they were planted, and the weather starts to turn, pull them out or cut at the base, and hang them somewhere dry and warm until the seeds dry completely, maybe one to two weeks. Then they're ready for harvest.

Both dill and cilantro seed can be harvested by cutting the heads into a container, then rubbing them with your hands to dislodge the seeds. Afterward, put them into zipper-lock plastic bags or plastic containers with lids (labelled and dated) and store them in a cool, dark, dry place. Yes, mason jars are more romantic, but if you drop it and the seed gets mixed with broken glass you may not be able to use it—and you definitely can't sell it. They're ready to plant the following year, and, voilà, you are a seed-saver!

Saving Seed: Parsley

Parsley is a biennial, which means it will only go to seed in its second year. Other common biennials are carrots, beets and anything in the onion family. To save parsley seed, leave the plants in the ground over the winter and lightly mulch them around the base to avoid frost damage. We use mulch hay (hay that hasn't gone to seed), but leaves can also work.

When last year's plants begin to grow again in early spring—before your new parsley plants have matured—you can harvest fresh parsley from them. (With so little fresh greens at this time of year, we really appreciate having access to fresh parsley!) When the centres of the plants start to grow tall, it's time to leave them in order to let the plant flower and set seed.

Leave them in the garden all summer, until the seeds are fully formed and dry (the dry seeds are dark in colour when ready). If late summer is wet, you can cut the plants and hang them indoors to dry. Rub the seeds off by hand into a container and put them in storage—again, in a cool, dark, dry place—ready to plant the following year.

LIZ

219

Q&A: *david*

DAVID FIRST MET Jennifer in 2003, and moved to the farm the following year. They live here with their two children, Alex and Rio. David is a California native who was introduced to Jennifer by his co-founding business partner, Alex Pryor. Over twenty years ago he and Alex started Guayakí, a company that sells organic, shade-grown and fairly traded yerba mate. David is responsible for the look, feel and story of Guayakí and he is committed to creating sustainable, life-generating enterprises that nourish the planet and humanity.

On the farm, David continues to help foster a culture of teamwork and mentorship, as well as helping the community clarify its vision and strategically accomplish its goals. He's also deeply passionate about music and has hosted many concerts on the farm.

You speak a lot about alignment and vision, especially when it comes to building teams. Can you elaborate on that?

All things great start with a vision. But as the vision grows beyond the founder, the biggest challenge is building a team to support the vision that has clear roles and responsibilities. For any individual to be part of a high-performing team, it's crucial to find the role that's best for you, one that suits your soul and who you are. Everyone has a certain genius and kind of a sweet spot to help it blossom. I believe that if people are committed to personal development, are supported to succeed and are in the right role—whether that's in an organization or community—they're more likely to thrive in that role and beyond it. Then they contribute to the success of everyone around them, and from there, it just keeps going and going.

One sign that you're not in the right role is that the same problems keep coming up, and you and the people you're with keep having the same dialogues about the same issues. If that's happening, maybe you need to re-examine the team, or the roles. It's so important for us as humans to have the experience of thriving in our roles.

What's something about life on the farm that you wish other people could experience?

It would be this experience of always having a deeper window into other people's lives. Not just in a professional setting, or a "best friend" setting, but in all the different layers of life. Whether it's at home, out working, at mealtime or doing events together, on the farm we all experience so many different parts of each other. From that you really start to understand who people are and where they're coming from. It gives a depth of relationship and connection that is really rare.

What do you think is so special about living on the farm?

Committing to live together like this is really going back to more of how tribes used to live together, with the exception that we now have a window into how the rest of the world lives—both the positives

and negatives. We are collectively and consciously creating the place we dream of and we want our kids to grow up in. We want it for ourselves, we want it for our kids, we want it for those who visit. And we want it as a model that people can look to for inspiration in these challenging times, where personal connection can be a lost art. On the farm, the beauty of the land and the built environment serves as the container for me—a constant reminder of what is sacred.

How has the farm impacted your personal life since moving away from the US to start life in a new country?

From day one, I was deeply moved by Stowel Lake Farm and the idea of everyone living together collaboratively and harmoniously on a shared piece of land. At one time, I had imagined living very simply in a rural setting, but living in community really pushed me to open up other parts of myself. Most of my adult life I have had the good fortune of having trusted and loved business partners at Guayakí. It was another dimension, however, to raise kids together with other families: merging

values, dreams, resources and sharing parenting in close quarters. While often confronted with challenges, the privilege of parenting with other trusted adults always provided more joy, stamina and strength to carry on and thrive. It is truly a wonder and unexplainable joy to see all of our kids playing endlessly together, running free wherever they may be.

How has the farm integrated with your life over time?

When I first moved to Stowel Lake Farm, I really had very few practical skills, like building or farming. Coming here, I was immediately surrounded by so many artistic and creative individuals, rooted on the farm and living on an island, pursuing passions different from my own. After getting my hands dirty in the field on our community work days and labouring on the building of my home, the creative juices were firing and I found myself diving back into music, a passion of mine which got sidelined when Alex and I started Guayakí. More than a decade later, I've transformed my workshop into a jam room where I practice with my band. And now I'm hosting music retreats for Come to Life (the media arm of Guayakí) on the farm to bring together everyone on the brand team with our artist-led music collective. And this year, 2018, will be the second year we are hosting our Guayakí companywide retreat on the farm—the ultimate integration of my personal and professional life.

This is an elegant autumn soup that fills the kitchen with the beautiful fragrances of pear, cinnamon and wine. Use ripe pears, and a nice rich squash variety such as kabocha, acorn or butternut. Serve with a crusty baguette or a rustic country loaf, maybe with some fresh goat cheese—and a simple salad that includes some bitter greens, like fresh arugula or radicchio. SERVES 6 TO 8

golden pear and
SQUASH SOUP

Heat oven to 375°F. Cut squash in half and remove seeds. Place squash on a parchment-lined baking tray and bake for one hour, or until soft. Let cool, scoop out the flesh and set aside.

Thinly slice pears, leaving skin on. Melt butter in soup pot over medium heat. Add pear slices and cinnamon. Sauté until fragrant and pears are tender (about 5 minutes). Add white wine, cover and simmer for 10 minutes, then add water and baked squash. Purée with immersion blender until smooth. Add optional cream, and salt and pepper to taste.

4 lb squash

6 large ripe pears

4 tbsp butter

2 tsp cinnamon

1 cup white wine

8 cups water

1 cup heavy cream (optional)

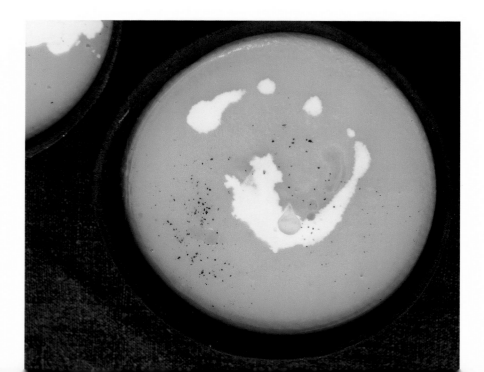

Minestrone is a classic Italian soup with a rich and varied history throughout Italy. I have fond memories of eating an excellent minestrone at a little trattoria in Montepulciano, served with country-style Tuscan bread on the side. This recipe begins with a soffrito: finely chopped carrot, onion and celery sautéed for half an hour to give the soup its depth of flavour. SERVES 4 TO 6

autumn harvest MINESTRONE

1 cup dried white beans
(or 1 796ml can cooked)

8 cups water

1 bay leaf

⅓ cup extra-virgin olive oil

1½ large onions

1 medium leek

3 garlic cloves

3 large celery stalks

4 medium carrots

1 zucchini

1 lb green beans

1 can (796ml) whole
plum tomatoes

1 bunch kale

½ head green cabbage

5 cups vegetable
stock (or water)

2 bay leaves

½ tsp red pepper flakes

1 tbsp salt (or to taste)

1 Parmigiano-Reggiano
cheese rind (optional)

1 cup grated Parmigiano-
Reggiano (optional)

The addition of autumn harvest vegetables such as tender green beans, zucchini, fresh cabbage and kale make this a hearty, nourishing soup. Here on the farm this is the soup that we most often bake in a pumpkin for serving as a festive dish around Halloween. For the beans, we like to use cannellini or other small white varieties.

Cover beans in water and soak overnight. Drain, add fresh water and bring to a boil with bay leaf and ½ an onion. Reduce heat and simmer, partially covered until tender (about 45 minutes). Strain beans and reserve cooking liquid.

For the soffrito, mince 1 stalk of celery, 1 medium carrot and 1 large onion. Set aside.

Heat olive oil in a large stock pot on low heat. Add minced soffrito vegetables and sauté, stirring occasionally, until deep golden brown (about 30 minutes).

Quarter the leek and slice ¼ inch thick; mince 3 garlic cloves. Chop remaining celery and carrots about ¼ inch thick; quarter and chop zucchini ¼ inch thick as well. Trim green bean ends and cut into pieces about 1 inch.

After the soffrito has reached a deep golden colour, add leek and garlic and cook, stirring often, for 5 minutes. Turn heat to medium-high and add celery, carrots, zucchini and green beans, stirring frequently until the vegetables are golden (about 6 to 8 minutes).

Stir in reserved bean liquid, tomatoes, kale, cabbage, stock, bay leaf, red pepper flakes, salt, pepper and optional cheese rind. Bring to a boil, then reduce to a simmer and cook, partially covered, for about 1 hour.

Add beans, simmer for another 30 minutes, and salt to taste. If you like, top with freshly grated Parmigiano-Reggiano before serving.

"Autumn harvest vege-
tables make this a hearty,
nourishing soup. Here
on the farm we often bake
it in a pumpkin for serving
as a festive dish around
Halloween."

HAIDEE

One thing I love to make for guests is a rustic cheese board. It's such a great, welcoming way to share food and to bring a sense of beauty into a social occasion. For me cheese boards are an ever-changing seasonal palette of flavours and colours, and they're another way to share my love of particular cheesemakers, olive growers, and all of the other inspiring producers around us.

about CHEESE BOARDS

THE CHEESE BOARD usually lives in the middle of my kitchen so that everyone can gather around it. There's a sense of breaking bread together at the beginning of a meal that is really special. Start with a good baguette and two or three cheeses from your local cheese shop or farmers market that you are excited about or interested in. If you can learn a little bit about the history behind a cheese and where it comes from, it's really enriching and special to share that with guests. It imparts a little excitement to everyone.

I usually include a medium-hard cheese, like a nicely aged cheddar or manchego. A big piece of Parmigiano-Reggiano or pecorino brings a lovely taste of the Italian countryside onto the board. I tend to put pretty big wedges out because they look so gorgeous. You can wrap what's left and keep reusing them.

A few of my favourite softer cheeses to serve are fresh chèvre, a double or triple cream cows' milk cheese, or a little dish of crème fraîche. Putting out a blue cheese such as stilton, Shropshire blue or gorgonzola gives a nice balance. Start with that foundation of three great cheeses and ensure they have some diversity of textures, flavours, age and appearance—and a little mix of goat, sheep, and cow.

I'm quite vegetable forward with these platters. In the spring I'll add a handful of brightly coloured radishes, or some fresh snap peas and pea shoots. In the summer I'll add lightly steamed green beans, cherry tomatoes and baby cucumbers. As soon as grape harvest begins in mid-September I start to add heaps of grapes and grape leaves, as well as fruit chutneys and preserves.

Finally, consider investing in a nice, rustic wooden board. The wood will develop a wonderful character over time, adding another lovely layer to the whole experience.

Brussels sprouts are enjoying a well-deserved comeback in the culinary world right now. This high-heat roasting method really brings out their sweetness and gives them a crispy texture around the edges. My daughter India will eat a huge bowl of these if given the chance! SERVES 6 TO 8

BRUSSELS SPROUTS
with maple-ginger glaze

Heat oven to 425°F. Trim off ends of the sprouts and cut in half, and finely chop the ginger. Melt butter on medium-high heat in a small pan. Add ginger and sauté until very fragrant (about 5 minutes). Add maple syrup and remove from heat.

Toss Brussels sprouts, olive oil and salt together in a large bowl. Spread onto large parchment-lined baking tray and roast for about 30 minutes, until golden and getting slightly crisp on the edges.

Remove Brussels sprouts from oven and gently toss to coat with maple syrup glaze. Place back in oven for another 5 minutes until golden brown. Enjoy hot or at room temperature.

4 lb Brussels sprouts

2 tbsp extra-virgin olive oil

1 tsp sea salt

2 tbsp butter

2 tbsp fresh ginger

2 tbsp maple syrup

Fifteen years ago there weren't many rabbits on Salt Spring, but now they are everywhere. This is a significant problem for the island's ecosystem. Part of my mission is to encourage people to cook foods that are underutilized or underrated, and rabbits are one of these—not only as wild game but also as an ethically raised meat source. They are also delicious! SERVES 4 TO 6

hunter style RABBIT STEW

One rabbit (3½ to 5 lb), bone-in and in pieces

3 tbsp extra-virgin olive oil

2 medium onions

3 tbsp chopped fresh rosemary

3 tbsp chopped fresh sage

2 to 3 cups red wine

1 can (796ml) whole tomatoes

1 to 2 cups water

Salt and pepper to taste

This recipe calls for one 3½- to 5-lb rabbit, as the size can vary. I find this dish is a bit different each time; sometimes saucier and sometimes meatier depending on the size of the rabbit.

This is a traditional cacciatore-style recipe, with those great Italian basics: red wine, good tomatoes and simple herbs like rosemary and sage that grow wild in the hills of Italy. It is traditionally served with polenta but we often pair it with Rosemary Sea Salt Mashed Potatoes (see page 271). You can also substitute chicken.

Rinse and pat dry bone-in rabbit pieces (leg, thigh, saddle, etc.). If you find rabbit through your local butcher, ask him to cut it into pieces for you. Cutting rabbit up is similar to cutting a chicken.

Lightly salt the rabbit pieces, and heat 3 tbsp olive oil in a large, heavy-bottomed, 5-quart casserole pot over medium-high heat. Brown pieces on all sides. Sear in batches to avoid crowding the pieces. Set all seared pieces aside.

Chop onions and herbs. Reduce heat to medium, and add to pan. Sauté until onions are golden brown (about 5 minutes).

Return rabbit pieces to pan and pour in 1 cup red wine. Cook over medium-high heat until all wine is evaporated, then scrape up brown bits on bottom of pot.

Pour whole tomatoes into a bowl and use your hands to break them up into small pieces. Add tomatoes to pan, along with the remaining red wine and about 1 to 2 cups water—enough to cover the rabbit by 2 inches. (If using 3½ lb of rabbit, use 2 cups of red wine— use up to 3 cups if using 5 lb of meat.)

Reduce heat to low, cover and simmer for about 25 minutes. Remove lid and boil for a few minutes to thicken the pan juices. Season with salt and pepper to taste. Serve over polenta or mashed potatoes, or on its own with a loaf of rustic bread.

We often serve risotto to our guests at the farm. It's such a fantastic vegetarian main dish that is truly seasonal—from an early spring version with fresh mint and asparagus to the deep autumn flavours of roasted squash and sage. I serve this particular risotto from late September into deep winter, as long as our winter squash lasts after pulling it in from the fields. SERVES 6 TO 8

squash and sage RISOTTO

Crispy sage leaves

4 tbsp extra-virgin olive oil

12 to 15 whole fresh sage leaves

Risotto

1 large butternut squash

3 tbsp extra-virgin olive oil

3 tbsp chopped fresh sage

2 cups arborio rice

10 to 12 cups vegetable stock

1 small onion, finely diced

⅓ cup dry white wine

2 tbsp butter

Coarse salt and
fresh black pepper

1 cup grated
Parmigiano-Reggiano

2 tbsp butter

I tend to use butternut squash for this recipe, but many other varieties, such as buttercup or kabocha, work well. (My favourite winter squash the past few years is a kabocha variety by the name of red kuri.) As with the Squash Blossom Risotto (see p. 104), this can be finished with butter, Parmigiano-Reggiano or even a little truffle oil.

Crispy sage leaves Heat 4 tbsp olive oil in a pan on medium heat. Add whole sage leaves and cook until fragrant and starting to crisp. This happens very quickly! It only takes about 30 to 45 seconds. You don't want the sage leaves to get too dark in colour. Remove with tongs and set aside on paper towel.

Risotto Heat oven to 375°F. Cut squash in half and remove seeds. Place on a parchment-covered baking tray and bake until soft (about 1 hour). Set aside to cool. When cool enough to handle, scoop the squash flesh out of the skin. Discard skin and set the cooked squash aside.

Heat vegetable stock and leave on a low simmer. It is important that stock is warm when you begin adding it to the risotto.

Dice onion and chop remaining 3 tbsp sage. Heat 3 tbsp olive oil in a large pot and sauté onion until translucent. Add rice and chopped sage and sauté, stirring, until rice starts to turn translucent (about 2 minutes). Pour in wine and cook just until liquid is absorbed. Begin adding stock to the rice, one ladleful at a time. Stir, until most of the liquid is absorbed. Continue adding stock, stirring with each addition.

When about halfway through adding stock, add cooked squash.
The squash will break up and blend in with the risotto as you continue
stirring and adding stock until the rice is tender. The rice should be
al dente but not crunchy, and the liquid should be creamy. It should
take about 25 minutes to get to this stage.

Add butter, season with salt and fresh pepper. Garnish with grated
Parmigiano-Reggiano (optional), fresh ground pepper and 2 to
3 crispy sage leaves per person.

This was my son Aliah's first birthday cake. I baked three large cakes and filled his little red wagon with them, all frosted and decorated with flowers. He's now 20, and still asks for this cake every birthday. I get many other requests for it: it's become a farm favourite. You can layer it and frost it, or you can keep it simple and serve it straight out of the oven for tea. This recipe is full of grated carrot, which results in a luscious, ultra-moist cake. This is also a great recipe to make with your favourite gluten-free flour blend. SERVES 8 TO 10

FARM CARROT CAKE
with cream cheese frosting

Cake Heat oven to 350°F. Butter two 8-inch round cake pans or one 9 × 12-inch pan. Combine carrot, pineapple and coconut in a large bowl and set aside.

   With an electric mixer, beat brown sugar with the eggs until tripled in volume. With mixer on low, add vanilla and slowly add oil until blended.

   Combine dry ingredients. First fold in the carrot mixture, then gently stir in the egg mixture. Divide batter between prepared pans and bake for about 30 minutes, until firm to the touch and a tooth-pick comes out clean when inserted. Remove from oven and let cool for 30 minutes before removing from cake pans.

Frosting Mix butter and cream cheese on high until light and fluffy. Turn mixer off, then add icing sugar, vanilla, lemon zest and juice. Mix on low until well combined. Place one cooled cake round onto a cake platter or large plate. Spread frosting on top of the cake round, then place second cake round on top and spread frosting evenly to cover the whole cake. I often garnish the finished cake with extra grated lemon zest and a handful of fresh berries for serving.

Cake

2 cups grated carrot

1 cup crushed pineapple

1 cup coconut

1 cup brown sugar

3 eggs

1 tsp vanilla

¾ cup vegetable oil

1½ cups unbleached white flour or gluten-free flour blend

2 tsp cinnamon

1 tsp baking soda

2 tsp baking powder

½ tsp salt

2 tsp dried ginger

1 tsp fresh nutmeg

Frosting

½ cup soft butter

1 package (454g) cream cheese

1 tsp vanilla

3 cups icing sugar

2 lemons, zest and juice

Every autumn I fall madly in love with this dessert. Packed with fresh ginger and molasses it's like an immune booster for the upcoming winter in the guise of a decadent dessert. SERVES 6 TO 8

FRESH GINGER CAKE
with pears

½ cup unsalted butter, room temperature

½ cup dark brown sugar

2 eggs

½ cup molasses

½ cup grated fresh ginger

1 tsp vanilla

½ cup milk

1½ cups flour (or 2 cups gluten-free mix)

½ tsp salt

1 tsp baking soda

3 to 4 pears

This cake is great with whipped cream after dinner, or served on its own with breakfast, lunch or tea. You can use apples or pears for the fruit; pears are my favourite, layered in the bottom of the pan so when you flip it upside down, you've got this lovely fruit on top. The recipe calls for a half-cup of grated fresh ginger. I find the easiest method is to process the ginger in a food processor or blender with a tiny bit of water added, so you don't lose any of the precious ginger juice.

Heat oven to 350°F and butter a 10-inch springform pan. Cream butter and sugar together for two minutes with an electric mixer, or by hand with a wooden spoon. Add molasses, ginger, eggs, vanilla and milk, and mix to combine.

Combine dry ingredients and add to butter-sugar mixture. Mix until just combined. Cover bottom of pan with a single layer of over-lapping pear slices. Spread batter over fruit. Bake for 35 to 45 minutes, until firm to touch and a knife inserted in middle comes out clean.

Allow to cool on rack for about 15 minutes, then run a knife around the springform pan and take the outer ring off. Hold a plate tightly to top of cake, flip upside down and gently loosen it from the bottom of the springform pan with a butterknife. Remove bottom of pan and place cake on plate or platter to serve.

DECEMBER

AS DECEMBER APPROACHES THE WEATHER changes into damp, windy days and we remember that we live in a rainforest. It's a time rich with the scent of mosses and balsam fir, along with pungent mud amid the beautiful puddles everywhere. We still work outside, but we are turning now toward celebrations of all kinds in this darkest of months. This is a big month of festive gatherings—I hope we are ready! The children certainly are, so we had better be. We start to bring the outside in, with boughs and berries, and it isn't long before we put up Christmas lights to illuminate our way.

It is a great opportunity to celebrate our ongoing respect and love for each other. We get a little of this every Thursday, but during the high season we are busy with our own concerns and responsibilities. Now we get to sit down more often with each other and catch up with feasts, games or rituals.

It's important to acknowledge that people of all ages live here: not so many elders, though more of these respected ones are finding us and enjoying their connection with different generations. Those in the middle—the parents, singles, thirtysomethings—all have so much to share and give. This mix, along with the children and young adults, keeps us all vital and aware. All year long we keep our connections

alive with singing, feasting, crafting, canning and telling stories together. It takes effort but the dividends are ongoing and very positive. It brings safety and stability to be a part of something that is bigger than the small self—it promotes comfort and joy for what is happening at this moment, and for the future.

On the Thursday before December 1, we pass around a basket with the names of each of the farmies who are going to be around for the month—along with a few members of our extended community—written on a paper slip. We all choose a person, adult or child, for whom we will be Secret Santa. Because the Barn is the central hub of the farm and we all go in and out of it daily, Santas leave their presents to be found there on a decorated dresser in the entry foyer. Everyone does their gift-giving differently, from very simple presents to funny things to fancy gifts, and the timing is completely random. The children check every day, pinching and prodding. It's a magic time.

A week or so before Christmas, we have our big holiday party, where the participants give their person a bigger present, and everyone guesses who their Secret Santa was all along. Farm Secret Santa brings us all a lot of joy and laughter and it's a great way to celebrate each person's special way of being in the world.

One interesting part of this celebration to me is that we also do some form of skit or song at this event—and, almost always, some folks come as each other and make jokes and give gentle ribbing about the characters with whom they spend so much time. In my readings about community and culture, it seems that this is one of the ways those who live so close together get to release tensions and frustrations in a skilful and humorous way. It seems to work well for us as a community, too, and it just came to be as we grew together. We all love this time of year.

LISA

246

the *farm* BOOKS

RECORD KEEPING IS an easy thing to overlook. When the busy farming season is done, we're all full of relief as the constant needs of the gardens slow down. Taking the time to reflect on what's just happened doesn't have the same urgency as harvesting, and the temptation is to let it slide. But recording what happened—when and what we planted, which crops thrived and which ones struggled—is vital to running a successful farm.

There are so many variables to track. Lisa once said that if a person can manage a diverse market garden, especially an organic one, they can manage (almost) anything.

When October arrives, however, it's difficult to remember how things were growing back in June. Because of this we have developed (and continue to improve) two important record-keeping books. One has all the seeding, transplanting and harvesting dates. This is where we document the varieties we've planted; make notes about crop failures, successes and pest issues; enter harvest weights; and add any ideas for improvement.

The second book is for sales records. Originally we had only one big book, but we now keep them separate: there were too many times when one farmer had the book down at the farmstand to note sales, while somebody else was in the midst of seeding and needed to write it down.

The books are meant to be used. There's no point discussing farming operations if you don't have any records, and there's no point keeping records if you don't have meetings to review them. If we know when the salad mix was planted, but there's no record of when it was harvested, or how much the planting produced, we have nothing to base next year's planning on, and farming becomes a guessing game. We've had years—too many of them!—where our record keeping was less than thorough, and from those years we've learned that if the information is only half there, it's actually not useful at all.

Throughout the growing season Liz, Meghan and I will get together a few times to review how the year is unfolding and look for solutions to any issues. At the end of the year we have a much more in-depth meeting, where we plan for the next season. This is the time when we look at bigger issues and consider our overall vision. We review the records and brainstorm ways to improve the farm operation—including apprentices, burnout and work environment—and explore ways the community can better support the farmers.

JEN

WINDOW *stars*

THERE ARE SO many festive, beautiful and creative things to do in December. For my family, I would have to take the whole month off to do it all. One thing I (almost) always make time for is making window stars with my kids. Here's how.

You'll need: Kite paper, glue sticks, tape (or something to stick them to the window). NOTE: You can use crepe paper, too; it's more fragile but often comes in more colours.

Folding

1 Choose 8 pieces of square paper (you can vary the colours to create a pattern).
2 Fold each sheet in half, then cut each along the fold to make 16 rectangles.
3 Fold each piece in half lengthwise, then unfold.
4 Take one piece and fold each corner to the centre line.
5 Fold each angle fold to the centre line, so you have a long diamond shape.
6 Repeat steps 4 and 5 for all 16 pieces.

Assembling

1 Lay out your folded pieces (according to your colour pattern, if you have one).
2 Make one end of the long diamond the bottom point, which will form the centre of the star. Place the bottom point of two folded pieces together, lining up the fold of one piece with the centre line of the other.
3 Use a glue stick to stick together. Repeat until you've created a 16-point star.
4 Place on a window and enjoy!

JEN

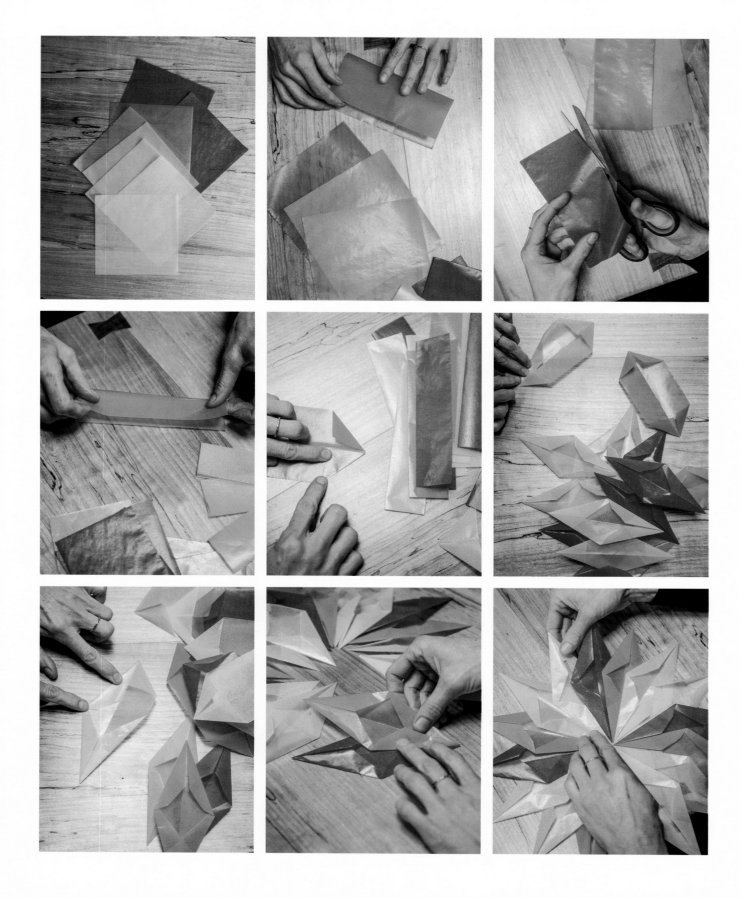

WINTER SOLSTICE

OUR SOLSTICE CELEBRATION is one of the most important events of our year. It's a chance to acknowledge our deep connection to the cycles of the Earth, and to honour the great turning of the wheel that is so much bigger than our little lives here on this land. We love to be a part of this age-old tradition of welcoming back the light, and it gives us a chance to welcome in our greater community.

Before the event we gather cedar and fir boughs from the land and lay them in a big spiral on the floor. We make candle-holders out of apples—which, after the celebration, the animals will eat—and practice the songs we're going to sing.

Then, on the solstice evening, friends and families come and join our community. We all arrive at the Gatehouse in silence, and enter the building in darkness. Upstairs we join in a circle and begin our evening. Families walk the spiral together while the singing goes on around. At the centre is a candle, which has been lit by the first walker in the spiral, always an elder. Each person lights his or her own candle from the centre, and for a moment each individual is the holder of the light. Then this person walks out of the spiral and finds a spot somewhere in the boughs to place their candle. And so it goes until everyone has had a turn.

At the end we sing everyone out with a farewell song, the candles are snuffed out and the silence stays intact until we are outside. At this point we head up to the barn to eat and drink and socialize. So many friends from our greater community come back year after year to share this time with us, which adds a special quality to the celebration. On good clear nights we have a fire in the courtyard, which ends the night in a very warm and lovely way.

LISA

FACING: Celebrating St. Nicholas Day is a sweet, yet simple, addition to early December. We put out our shoes at night and St. Nick fills them with fruit, nuts, chocolate coins, and beeswax candles. Decorating with greenery gives a sense of abundance and beauty.

RIGHT: Handmade holiday cards are easy and fun for anyone to create. This technique uses rubber stamps and all the supplies are available at art stores.

Q&A: *Matt*

MATT GREW UP rural, on five acres of forested land on southern Vancouver Island. He was always interested in the outdoors, and in his early twenties he studied adventure tourism in Kamloops and spent a few summers in the BC Interior as a forest firefighter. While in school he met Liz and joined her and Jennifer in leading kayak trips in the summers, spending his winters as a downhill ski patroller and operations manager. After further studies he joined the faculty of Vancouver Island University, where he now teaches courses and leads trips in the Outdoor Recreation program.

Matt moved to the farm after a few years of visiting Liz and participating in whatever farm activities were happening. After their first baby was born, they started to build a house on the property, where they are now raising their three children, Addie, Max and Scout. Matt loves backcountry skiing, surfing, mountain biking and kayaking, and still gets his fair share of chainsaw time bucking firewood.

The lifestyle and setting on the farm seem to suit your love of physical, outdoor activity.

Farming anywhere is going to be hard work, whether you're a potato farmer in Idaho or you're doing grain in Saskatchewan. Even if it's highly mechanized, it's still giant hours and huge days. Bring it all the way back to an organic farming approach of pulling individual weeds, and it just takes a ton of labour. What I've always appreciated about the farm is that the results of your efforts here are measurable. You know what you've accomplished.

It's very different from the kind of work most of us have, where the measure is not so visible or tangible. It can be as simple as, "Hey Matt, we need you to weed the strawberries." So you go out, do a morning of weeding, and by noon, there it is: maybe half a row, two rows, whatever you did. Or bucking up a huge pile of firewood and getting it all nicely stacked. Of course the weeds come back, and the firewood gets burned, but there it is: in this moment of time, there is my measure.

Talk about the scholarship program that you helped start on the farm.

This place is great because it's small enough that good ideas will be listened to, and can move forward rapidly. The scholarship program was one of those good ideas that took off because people were interested and there was a way for it to happen. It started because Lisa and I had a chance to attend a five-day Soulcraft workshop held on the farm by the Animas Valley Institute. It was something I wouldn't have otherwise done, but I was offered the chance to attend, so I went. I was profoundly moved by it. It helped me in all sorts of aspects in my life, and was hugely beneficial.

Afterward I thought: "We all need to do this. The people who live here should all get to have these sorts of experiences." So I came up with this idea that whoever wanted to participate would pay twenty dollars a month into a shared pot. Every year the money would be disbursed to someone for a personal growth workshop or development experience of some sort. There are seven of us who've been doing it the past seven years, generating about $1,700 annually, and it's been awesome, giving all of us the chance to have a potentially life-changing experience.

Why do you think the farm has been able to thrive and evolve over the years into such a successful business and community?

One of the more interesting things about living in community is that stuff comes out, and you can't hide. You can't hide who you are, and if it's a pretty switched-on group of people, which this group is, you get called on your stuff. Not in a destructive way, but in the best way. People are interested in you. You see them, they see you, and everyone is encouraged and given the space to grow into the best person they can be.

It doesn't mean it's not messy or it doesn't hurt, or that you don't want to throttle someone sometimes. But at the root of it, and the real reason why things work so well here, is love. People really love and care for each other, and that's talked about openly. In our society we're generally quite scared to use that word. You can care about someone you know, in your workplace or wherever, but do you actually love them? And really the answer is yes, you do. But we don't talk that way because it's too scary, too loaded. So if people are calling you on your stuff here, that's the root: it's because you've lived with them for fifteen to twenty years and they love you deeply. That's the foundation, the root of community on the farm.

In the late fall on the farm we start embracing the hardier greens that overwinter here in our climate. We grow many different varieties of kale which can be combined or used interchangeably in most recipes. If the plants are well established enough in late summer, they can last all through the winter, and after the first few frosts the kale becomes sweeter and more flavourful. SERVES 4 TO 6

KALE *salad*

In this salad, massaging the kale with the acidic lemon juice or vinegar essentially cooks it while maintaining all of the nutrients—it becomes tender, and a really gorgeous dark green. My children eat huge bowlfuls of this salad. Bragg's seasoning noted in the ingredients is gluten-free and I use it in place of soy sauce and tamari in most of my recipes.

Wash kale and remove tough stems. Tear or chop kale finely and place in salad bowl. Mix together olive oil, lemon juice or vinegar, and tamari or Bragg's.

    Pour dressing over kale, then massage into the kale, squeezing handfuls until the kale leaves start to wilt and darken in colour. Before serving, add toasted seeds and optional finely chopped apple or pear.

12 cups kale

¾ cup extra-virgin olive oil

½ cup fresh lemon juice or apple cider vinegar

½ Bragg's or ⅓ cup tamari or soy sauce

1 cup toasted sunflower, pumpkin or sesame seeds

1 to 2 apples or pears (optional)

265

Cauliflower is a humble vegetable that seems to be finally getting the attention it deserves. This is a really tasty recipe, and the key is to let the cauliflower begin to get very dark brown. You can serve this dish warm or cold, and it's also delicious if you omit the Indian spices and just use olive oil and salt. My kids really love this dish. You can serve it as part of an Indian meal, but it also goes so well with just about every flavour in this book. SERVES 6 TO 8

ROASTED CAULIFLOWER
with indian spices

2 large cauliflower heads

5 tbsp extra-virgin olive oil

½ tsp cumin

½ tsp coriander

½ tsp turmeric

1 tsp salt

1 bunch parsley (optional)

Heat oven to 450°F. Cut cauliflower in half, removing the tough core stem. Break cauliflower florets into a mix of different sizes; having a variety of shapes and sizes gives the finished dish great texture. In a large bowl, toss cauliflower with olive oil, salt and spices. Spread florets on a baking tray and bake for 25 to 35 minutes, until they turn brown and very fragrant. Transfer to a serving platter and, if you like, garnish with roughly chopped parsley.

There are many nights throughout the year when a simple, flavourful roast chicken is the perfect dinner for everyone. We raise our own chickens on the farm, so there is an aspect of pride in being able to share our beautiful poultry with friends and loved ones. SERVES 4 TO 6

roast farm CHICKEN

1 large free-range chicken (4 lb)

4 tbsp + 1 tbsp soft butter

4 tbsp fresh
rosemary or tarragon

2 tsp salt

2 tsp freshly ground pepper

Roasting chicken can be easier and less stressful than turkey! For larger dinners we will sometimes roast two or three of these chickens in a nice big pan and there is always enough for everyone. The trick to keeping these birds moist and flavourful is to tuck a layer of fresh herb butter between the skin and the breast. The herbs are flexible; I list rosemary and tarragon here but feel free to try fresh thyme, oregano, sage or a combination of your favourites.

I often serve this roasted chicken with basmati rice or Perfect Crispy Potatoes (see page 316), braised kale, and green salad with a basic vinaigrette (see Jennifer's Vinaigrette, page 71).

Heat oven to 400°F. Rinse chicken and pat dry with paper towel. Mince fresh herbs and mix in small bowl with 4 tbsp butter. Place chicken in roasting pan. Carefully separate skin of chicken from the breast, starting above the open cavity of the chicken. This can be done gently with your hands or, if necessary, with a small paring knife. You just want to separate a few inches of the skin so that you can tuck the soft herb butter between the skin and the breast. It's very important that the skin stays attached along the sides and isn't taken right off.

Gently tuck the herb butter in between the skin and breast, and rub the additional tablespoon of butter over the outside of the chicken. Sprinkle salt and pepper over the whole chicken and place in oven. Roast for approximately 1 hour, until golden brown and the temperature reaches 140°F when tested deep in the thigh area of the chicken with a meat thermometer.

Remove chicken from oven and let rest for 10 to 15 minutes. I tent the chicken with foil and lay a tea towel over it to keep warm. This resting process allows the juices of the chicken to evenly distribute throughout the bird. To serve, I usually carve the chicken and set the pieces back into the roasting pan with the roasting juices.

Infusing good organic cream or milk with rosemary is the key to this recipe. The herb-infused cream simmers while the potatoes cook, and by the time the potatoes are done you end up with this herbaceous, gorgeous flavour that you add into the mashed potatoes. I love to finish these with a sprinkle of coarse sea salt. SERVES 4 TO 6

rosemary sea salt
MASHED POTATOES

Wash potatoes. If organic, there is no need to peel them. Cut in half, place in a large pot and cover with cold water to about 2 inches above potatoes. Bring to a boil, then lower heat to medium and cook for 15 to 20 minutes, until potatoes are soft when pierced with a fork.

Finely chop rosemary and add to milk or cream in a small saucepan. Heat to just before the boiling point. Lower heat to a simmer simmer while potatoes cook.

Drain the potatoes well and return them to pot. Add butter and mash well, then add rosemary-infused cream and continue mashing until smooth. Salt and pepper to taste.

4 lb Yukon gold potatoes

1 cup milk or cream

4 tbsp finely chopped rosemary

½ cup butter

1 tbsp sea salt, or to taste

Coarse sea salt and pepper

Not only is this traditional Christmas recipe very festive and beautiful, it's also relatively easy to make. Jennifer and Liz are usually the ones who make it at the farm at Christmas and we all get to enjoy it together. The tradition comes from Liz's family, and we are so happy that she has shared it with all of us. It's fun to decorate and the cake itself is flourless, which goes over well with everyone these days. SERVES 8

liz's BUCHE DE NOEL

Chocolate cream

2 cups whipping cream

½ cup icing sugar

½ cup unsweetened cocoa powder

1 tsp vanilla extract

Sponge cake

6 eggs, yolks and whites separated

½ cup + ¼ cup white sugar

⅓ cup unsweetened cocoa powder

1½ tsp vanilla extract

⅛ tsp salt

Icing sugar for dusting

Chocolate cream In a large bowl, whip cream with icing sugar, cocoa and vanilla until thick and stiff. Refrigerate.

Sponge cake Heat oven to 375°F. Line a 10 × 15-inch rimmed baking sheet with parchment paper. Prepare a clean tea towel by liberally dusting it with icing sugar—this will be for turning the cake out onto when it comes out of the oven. Set towel aside.

To make the cake, use an electric mixer to beat egg yolks with ½ cup sugar until smooth and pale in colour. Mix in cocoa, vanilla and salt.

In a separate bowl, whip egg whites until soft peaks start to form. Continue beating and slowly add ¼ cup sugar, beating until the whites form stiff peaks. Add yolk mixture into whites and gently fold together. Spread batter into the pan and smooth it out so it is fairly flat.

Bake for 12 to 15 minutes, or until cake springs back when lightly touched. Turn warm cake out onto the sugar-dusted tea towel and carefully remove parchment paper from the cake. Starting at its shorter edge, roll cake with the towel so that it cools while taking the shape of the log. (Be sure to roll a short log, rather than a long one!) Allow it to cool.

To finish Unroll the cake and spread half of the chocolate cream on the cake. Roll cake up with filling inside. Place seam side down onto a platter and spread rest of the chocolate cream over the outside of the log. You can use a fork or other sharp tool to make bark-like lines on the cake. Refrigerate.

Just before serving, dust with powdered sugar and decorate with holly or other winter greenery.

This is a classic French dessert with lots of wonderful mythology around it. It goes back to the late 1800s, to a small hotel in the village of Lamotte-Beuvron. Allegedly the Tatin sisters who ran the hotel accidentally dropped an apple tart, and out of desperation tried to rescue it—but they cooked it upside down. When they took it out they discovered the lovely caramelization that is the really incredible part of this dessert. SERVES 8

TARTE *tatin*

6 medium-large apples (about 3 lb)

½ cup + 8 tbsp cold unsalted butter

1¼ cups unbleached white flour

1 cup +1 tsp sugar

1 tsp salt

3 to 4 tbsp cold water

2 cups heavy cream, whipped (optional)

I begin to make this dessert in early fall, using heritage apples that will hold their shape, like Cox's Orange Pippin or Gravenstein. Note that this recipe is made for a deep, heavy skillet (cast iron works best) that measures 7 to 8 inches across the bottom and 10 to 11 inches across the top.

Heat oven to 375°F. Place flour in a food processor. Cut ½ cup of cold butter into 1-inch pieces and add to food processor along with 1 tsp sugar and 1 tsp salt. Pulse briefly until mixture forms pea-sized pieces. This happens quickly! (This can also be done by hand in a mixing bowl using two knives or a pastry blender to combine the ingredients.) Add cold water, a small amount at a time, and pulse until dough holds together. You may not need to add all of the water, or you may need a little extra. If you over-process at this point the pastry will be tough, so mix just until it holds together.

Turn dough out onto lightly floured counter. Roll out into a 12-inch circle. Transfer dough to a cookie sheet and refrigerate.

Peel, core and quarter the apples lengthwise. Heat a heavy skillet on medium-high heat. Add 8 tbsp butter, melt, and remove skillet from heat. Sprinkle 1 cup sugar evenly over melted butter, covering bottom of pan. Arrange apples in a concentric circle, filling in the middle with additional pieces. Pack as tightly together as possible until bottom of pan is covered.

Return skillet to medium-high heat. Cook for about 8 to 10 minutes, until sugar and butter under the apples have turned a deep amber colour and apples are turning golden brown on the cooked side. Remove from heat and use a fork to carefully turn each piece of apple

over. Return to heat and cook on medium-high for 5 minutes more. Watch carefully so as not to burn the butter-sugar mixture. Remove from heat once again and slide prepared pastry over the apples, carefully (the pan is hot!) tucking edges of pastry around edges of apples against the inner sides of the skillet.

Place in oven and bake for 30 to 35 minutes, until crust is golden brown. Remove from oven and set aside to cool for about 20 minutes. Loosen edges of the pastry with a knife, and invert carefully onto a serving plate. If any apples stay in the pan, just loosen them and tuck them back into their place, along with any extra caramel from the bottom of the pan. Delicious served with freshly whipped cream.

A French classic from the 1800s, created by two sisters who ran a small provincial hotel. Allegedly they cooked an apple tart upside down by accident—only to discover the lovely caramelization that makes this dessert so special.

DEEP WINTER

RAINING, SNOWING OR COMPLETELY freezing, deep winter is all about the chill outside and the warmth inside by the hearth. Every day, no matter what, I'll seize the opportunity to take a nice long walk.

Passing by the Gatehouse I'm greeted by a most powerful scent— this surprise is sarcococca, a shade-loving plant that flowers in late January against the sheltered building. Snowdrops are coming up, and the witch hazel and Cornus mas are putting out their curly yellow flowers. At this latitude on the West Coast the garden goes to sleep for such a short time.

Despite the brisk and sometimes bleak conditions, the birds are still with us. Robins are thronged in the crabapples, eating the frozen berries. The chickadees are often down on the forest floor, searching in groups for food. There are ravens and hawks above, and winter ducks in the ponds. It's a lovely time for taking pictures. With the sun's reflection on frozen puddles many small and beautiful vistas come together. Sometimes all of us slide around on the thick ice of the lake and see our world from a very different perspective.

The days are lengthening now that winter solstice is past, but they are still so short. Every morning I like to make a plan for any outside work because darkness comes early and there can easily be more to do. I prepare the greenhouse for the spring, make my seed order and reassess the seeds that I collected in the fall.

These few weeks of deep winter are a chance to give oneself the gift of quiet, introspection and self-care. For most of the year, our farm lives are social; this is a chance to pull away from all that and to see what emerges from the depths of our beings. Contemplation. What a lovely gift. Not to be trifled with.

We all need this inner time, and I give thanks to the enclosing darkness and cold. Sometimes I would like to hibernate as the bears do and just spend time dozing and remaking myself. This is definitely a time of rejuvenation and renewal—a time to feel the seeds germinating in oneself for the passions of the seasons to come.

LISA

WINTER VEGETABLES

Freshly dug winter carrots are miles beyond those bags of organic carrots at the store. They're sweet, crunchy, full of flavour and alive. Harvesting them in the middle of winter is usually cold and dirty work, but it's always satisfying. When it's freezing or snowy, we have to peel back a stiff layer of mulch in order to see the rows of carrots still hunkered down in the earth, and use a garden fork to loosen the frozen soil so we can pull them out.

There is something gratifying about eating your own vegetables throughout the winter, whether they're in storage or out in your garden. Along with carrots, we harvest beets, spinach, leeks and January King cabbages from the garden in the colder months. There are also lots of hardy kale varieties that overwinter well and are so sweet when the temperatures drop a bit, like Red Russian kale and winterbor. We keep our potatoes, squash and garlic in storage and grab them whenever we need them.

There are a few tricks to keeping vegetables in the garden over the winter. In mid to late fall, before the first frost, we cut the tops off the beets and carrots, leaving about an inch or so, and then bury them in a six-inch layer of seedless mulch hay. This keeps them from freezing, unless we get an unseasonably cold winter, where temperatures drop below minus 5 for days at a time.

Leafy greens such as spinach and kale don't tend to last outside all winter, so we always plant a few in our greenhouses to get a little season extension. Some plants will die over the winter, but the ones that don't start growing again in early spring.

LIZ

thoughts on COMMUNITY

A FEW DAYS AGO our three cows got out and went running past the house—and who was going to do something about that? The thing about our cows is that they are never convenient. They really like to be out on Sunday mornings, or at dinnertime, for example. Luckily one of the guys around got excited about it, and encouraged the kids to get big branches and flail them about in the air, which the kids loved, and this activity encouraged the cows to return to their pasture. Mission accomplished, and it was fun, too.

We're fortunate to have a community of people here who will jump in when needed, and take care of what needs to get done for the common good. A belief in that kind of commitment is an essential element of making life work in a small community where everyone has a lot of responsibility. In some vital way we need to look out at the world together, with the same philosophy, and for us, that outlook is caring for the land, and for all the beings that live here.

Over the years this farm and our little community have selected for these people, people who genuinely care as much, or more, about the greater good than about themselves.

"You've got to serve somebody," Bob Dylan once sang. And Gandhi lived his conviction that you've got to be willing to do every job, from cleaning toilets to managing. I have been and still am so influenced by these approaches to life. I deeply believe them to be a good and true way to live. Service doesn't involve giving oneself away: instead, it's an approach to life that takes the whole into consideration.

On the farm we talk so much about the common good, and many times we fail, but when this idea permeates our discussions about any subject, it brings a bigger perspective to the conversation. We believe most things are possible, but it takes this understanding, this big view, to help it along.

LISA

LEFT: Nicola & Jennifer creating a winter bouquet.
FACING: Lisa & Alex putting the echeverias to bed.

I work in the perennial garden at
the farm and arrange retreat flowers.
I'm fortunate to love my work, love
the people I work for and love the
community. There's autonomy and
reciprocity in the relationship, which I
highly value. The life here is of goodness,
and I have the opportunity to participate
and contribute to what's created here.
And then there are the children, two
handfuls of them: joy-filled, delightful,
happy and healthy. I love them to bits.
They bring laughter and play into my
life, which is a gift indeed.

NICOLA

Retreats are a big part of our
life and business on the farm.
We host hundreds of guests
every year who gather here for
yoga and meditation retreats,
wellness programs, dance and
music workshops, and more.

Inside the Gatehouse:
our much-loved retreat
space gets used for a wide
variety of programs.

ABOVE: Cozy living room area,
upstairs in the Barn.

FACING, CLOCKWISE FROM TOP LEFT:
A retreat room in one of our yurts; the Gatehouse
at night; the Gatehouse entrance; chairs in the
garden for rest and enjoyment.

292

YURT *program*

FOR THE PAST four years, our educational programs on the farm have served about twenty-five Salt Spring children ranging in age from six to fourteen. The classes are held in a large yurt. Students practice reading, writing and math with the teacher and they also get to experience a variety of opportunities with other instructors in karate, music, drama and art. One day a week they learn about biology, forest ecology and ecosystems with (very overqualified) local biologists by wandering the farm and other places on Salt Spring. The yurt also gets used by kids in the WOLF program— a nature connection and awareness curriculum— for their academic studies.

On the farm we're fortunate to have the space, inside and outside, to hold everything from weekly martial arts classes to Christmas concerts for young people. We're delighted to have the farm be a part of so many kids' lives.

The origin of the yurt school started with my son Alex years ago. We were seeking a program that would give him the best chance to thrive when he started Grade 1. After a lot of thought we decided to create our own program on the farm. With his tutor at the time, Amy Caesar—who became our first teacher—we discovered a distributed learning program that funded alternative educational approaches. Starting this program was a risk for the parents, kids and teachers involved, and the results have been tremendous.

One highlight comes during spring break in March. It's by far the favourite week of the year for the kids, but not because they get a break from learning. In fact, it's the opposite! "Workshop Week" runs for up to five days, and kids sign up for three or four classes every day: sewing, archery, print-making, hiphop dance, business skills, carpentry, book-making, music, cooking, mapping and making fairy houses in the forest are all options. The classes are mostly taught by parents who volunteer to teach anything in which they are "experts." There is so much hidden talent out there.

One year my son Rio made a book during Workshop Week; he was so proud that he entered it into the local Salt Spring Island Fall Fair. Another year one of the mothers taught a class called "Small Engine Investigation." She brought old appliances (vacuums, blenders, toasters, et cetera) that the kids took apart with tools in order to learn how they worked. The kids raved about it.

JEN

THE FARM *kids*

Addie Kellow, 12

It's really fun to live so close to my friends and to be able to hang out together. In the summer we ride bikes, play tag in the perennial garden and play soccer. In the winter there's awesome sledding up the road, and also right where we live, off our deck.

Because everything's so close, when I'm over at Alex and Rio's and I want to go home, it's not like I have to call my mom or dad and ask them to drive over and pick me up. I can just walk home any time I want.

Generally I like living around a bunch of people that I've known my whole life. I know them really well and I can trust them and we have a lot of fun.

Alden Demandre, 8

Usually, when my dad's working, I go to find him and then eventually go up to Alex and Rio's to play. We go to see the bunnies. You can pick them up, and it's fun. We go to the hillside and play hide and seek, or we play in the hay bales.

If I can't find the other kids, I hang out with my dad and I get to work in the shop with him. When we are working on a project, Papa uses the machines and I use the glue gun or carve with a knife.

Also, I think it's kind of cool that I can just dig up a carrot and eat it.

Alex Lloyd-Karr, 10

My favourite foods to eat when I'm walking around the farm are cucumbers, tomatoes, carrots and peas. When I take a walk down to the gardens to get some vegetables to eat, I'll see Meghan or Thea. Meghan is always picking tomatoes, and it's fun because then I'm not the only one out there, and we can talk about anything.

I have two cats, Milo and Anjou. Anjou is fussy and very smart—he can open the doors to our house. Sometimes I come home from school and our front door is wide open. Anjou is a Siamese and Milo is a ginger.

I love growing succulents. My favourite is a really big agave that I got for Easter—it's really poky, not like a cactus, more like an aloe vera. I love to talk about these plants with Granny, who gave me my first one.

Aliah Hart, 20

Growing up here was this experience of just having so many rad people around all the time to talk to and ask different questions. Outside of my family, I've had quite strong relationships with all the guys on the farm, like Matt and David. They've kind of been that uncle role. You get all these outside points of view that are a little removed from, and different than, those of your blood family. It's really a sweet spot.

Another thing about growing up on a farm is that you're not sheltered. If you're raising animals, kids should be able to see the whole circle of it, not just the cute phase, but everything, including how they become food. From that I really learned to give thanks. To animals and even to trees I cut down, as an acknowledgment, a sign of respect.

Atisha Roach Lloyd, 15

I live out on Isabella Point Road, on the other side of Fulford Harbour. I come to the farm to visit family—Lisa, Jennifer, David and the boys—and to play games, have fun and just be with the community in the different celebrations together.

I think the farm is absolutely wonderful because the kids all have such a deep, loving connection with nature. It's not so much watching TV and that kind of thing. They all want to play outside, or write in their journals or play board games, because that's what they've been brought up with.

Aurelia Demandre, 10

I like running around the farm and picking vegetables for lunch. Carrots and peas are my favourites. When we're pulling weeds on Thursdays I like that, too, because some of them are edible.

I love seeing the bunnies. My favourite is Amanda. She's white with black spots and a black stripe down her back.

I play with India, Max and Addie a lot, and in the summertime sometimes we play in the apple orchard or the perennial garden. And we all run in the sprinklers they use to water the plants. All the kids are like, "Aaaaa, the sprinklers are going off!"

Hanna Borkowska Kirk, 13

There's a lot of space and a lot of people to hang out with around the farm. Everyone does their own thing, but everyone's really connected, too. We live at the back of the property so I can be there by myself, or I can come up to the Barn and hang out with everybody. I like that.

The farm is also a great place to learn. On Wednesdays some friends and I do an independent study on the farm called Kamana, a naturalist training program. The last time we did it, we did the "Tourist Test," which asks questions about the wilderness and animals here. Some are really tricky, like: "What's one tree that's safe to hide under during a windstorm that won't snap off and fall on you?"

India Hart, 8

One cool thing on the farm is that you don't have to wear shoes, even in the winter. And you have so much room, not just a tiny backyard. You have everywhere.

The kids ride bikes to each other's houses, and we play on the swing set, or go see the animals, like Spike the llama and Santana the alpaca, and the bunnies. And the chickens. You can pick the chickens up if you get their wings tucked in. My favourite is named Beauty, she's kind of reddish brown.

I also spend a lot of time in the barn kitchen with my mom, and with Thea and Meghan in the farm room or the garden, or at their houses.

Jacob Hart, 13

I'd spend hours running around the farm with the other kids when I was younger, sword fighting and playing in the perennial garden, or up on the hillside, especially after the swales got put in. Addie and Max and I had some good times up there.

Music is a big thing for me now and it's added a whole new aspect for me to meet and spend time with the musicians who come to the farm, like Rising Appalachia and Dustin Thomas. Not just to see them perform, but to be with them when they're jamming, or spend some bonding time with them—that's just been super amazing.

Lulu Lee, 10

I live just up the road, and I come to play with the kids here a lot. We'll go to the cow barn and climb around the hay bales, or come to the main barn and play. They taught me how to climb up on the beams, which was really fun.

The celebrations are all so fun here, too. I really love the solstice spiral, where we do the spiral walk with our apple candles, and then it's all calm, and everyone's singing. And at the end you can take your apple and eat it.

Maxwell Kellow, 10

On Thursdays I like to work in the garden, pulling weeds usually, or digging potatoes. As the tractor parts the soil, the potatoes pop up behind it. Kids dig them out and all the adults put them in buckets, and it's really fun.

Also, soccer in the evening in the summer is cool. Usually what happens is either David, Alex, Rio, Addie or I call over to each other's houses and ask if the others want to come play after dinner. We play in Alex and Rio's front yard. It's a time that we get to be together, and I like sharing time with those guys.

I really like how all of our families are emotionally and physically close. I can go to anyone's home and I'll be welcomed.

Noah Hart, 16

All the people on the farm are parent figures to me, including Jen and David, Liz and Matt and Lisa. Everyone has played a big part in my upbringing.

Growing up on the farm has had such a positive effect on my childhood and I've really benefitted from all the opportunities I've had.

I was homeschooled until about the eighth grade and during that time I had a lot of independence. Having so much time on my hands I got really into birdwatching with Daphne, who works in the perennial garden—it was amazing. After a year of doing it, I really started to notice the little things, like if the barn swallows were a week late to return due to a late frost.

I spent a lot of time working on the farm doing tractor work and odd jobs, like finding a cow that had broken through a fence and had gone for a stroll down the road. I raised a cow myself when I was thirteen. It was super fun, but the cow would only listen to me. By two months old it was a couple of hundred pounds and they'd have to come get me to tell it to move out of the garden.

Rio Lloyd-Karr, 8

Summer solstice is one of my favourite things. That's when everyone goes down to the lake field to camp out and roast marshmallows and hot dogs. We all play fun games like sack racing and three-legged racing and all that kind of stuff.

I also like going all around the farm on the golf cart, maybe doing the compost or putting stuff in the burn pile, or just giving Isela rides around the farm to pick flowers.

Another cool thing is when Scout, Alex and I make pictures for Romi, and Romi makes pictures for us. You go to the mailbox and see a picture waiting in there for you, or you put a picture in the mailbox for him.

Scout Kellow, 6

I love everything about the farm! In the summer I float in the lake in my life jacket, and I eat lots of stuff in the gardens, like those little orange tomatoes.

In winter I like how beautiful all the trees look when it's snowing.

And I like the cows. We named them Boss and Oreo Cookie. I go down there with Rio and Alex and Max and Alden. There's a fence in the barn and I stick my hand through and feed them hay sometimes.

LISA DESCRIBES ROMAN'S arrival on the farm this way: "He walked up the driveway one day twenty years ago and never left." Born in Poland, Roman moved to Canada in 1984, eventually settling in Montreal. In the mid-nineties he worked as a seasonal apple picker, and season after season a fruit-picking friend named Jean would talk about a West Coast island he loved to visit called Salt Spring.

In 1997 Roman bought a cross-country bus ticket and came out to see for himself. At the time, Jean was living on Stowel Lake Farm, and through some lucky coincidences Roman was able to find him here. And, indeed, he never left! He's done many jobs on the farm, from construction labour to weeding to permaculture plantings. Along with making big batches of homemade sauerkraut, one of his favourite occupations is working with the farm children in their shared tradition of exchanging drawings and paintings.

You talk about your "lucky star" bringing you to Stowel Lake Farm. What's the story behind that?

Coming here for me was definitely the effect of my lucky star. First of course there was meeting Jean, and learning about Salt Spring. But when I got to the island I had no idea where he was. At the time Jean's girlfriend was a waitress at a restaurant in Fulford, and I'd gotten off the ferry and was walking by the restaurant with my big backpack. You know how busy waitresses are, but for the five seconds I was passing the restaurant window she happened to look out and see me. She ran out to talk to me, told me that Jean was at Stowel Lake Farm, and gave me the address, and I walked from the ferry terminal to the farm.

I ended up not coming to the right place, and a neighbour showed me a way to get in through a hole in the fence, and there was Jean's Volkswagen van right there—parked at the time about ten feet away from where I live in my yurt right now. So in twenty years I've moved about ten feet. All of it was like that lucky star was guiding me. If she hadn't looked through the window and seen me, my life could look totally different right now.

What is it about life here on the farm that made you decide to stay?

It's a mix of so many things. Of course because of Lisa there was a job for me here, but it's not just because of the work. Lisa is that kind of person who you know you can count on. In the middle of the night, or whatever day of the week it might be, I know that she would be there for me, and vice versa. There's a very strong and unique friendship between us.

There is also just living in this place, with the excitement I'd never had in my life before of being so close to nature. Some people go on vacation in a beautiful place and snap photos so they can remember it. Here, every single day of my life is like that. I've had it over two decades. This yurt that I live in—a yurt is a tent, to be honest, so every day is like camping. Keeping myself warm with firewood in winter, sleeping outside in a hammock in summer. No traffic, just birds and nice people walking by. The walls are so thin that sometimes I'll hear a big owl and jump off my bed because of the sudden sound in the deep silence.

Talk about the art exchange you have with the farm kids.

Being single and being at the middle of a community surrounded by families, it's very nice. I love Montreal, and I have great memories there, but I wouldn't have had the same thing with my neighbours and their kids there. I like kids very much. They have this spirit that's just amazing. The kids here, they come very often to see me, to say hello, and we exchange drawings. It's one for one: I draw one for them and they draw one for me. I like abstract very much, and I try to develop in them this way, kind of, of seeing things through abstraction.

They always want to share with me what they drew the evening before. One Saturday, at 7:30 in the morning, they knocked on my door—Scout, Alex and Rio—with new drawings they were excited to show me. I was sleeping, and it woke me up when I heard someone walking up the driveway. I'm thinking, "What's going on? What's going on?" Then I see it's the kids, and a few minutes later they show me their drawings. I was so happy, so happy. So that's a really enormous plus. Families and their kids, I love it.

This is one of our family's most frequently-made winter salads.
I love the combination of fennel, apple and lemon with cabbage—
the simple, fresh ingredients come together to create a
brightly flavoured salad with great texture. SERVES 6 TO 8

winter fennel, apple and
CABBAGE SALAD

Cabbages, like kale, become sweeter with the cold. It's pretty magical
to walk out to the garden in the winter and harvest a cabbage out
from under the snow. We try to grow enough cabbages on the farm
to keep us all supplied year-round as it is such a great staple; our
favourite variety at the moment is the January King, which keeps
incredibly well through the colder months.

Salad Finely shred cabbage (a mandolin works very well), dice the
fennel and its greens, and thinly slice the apples.

Dressing Zest and juice the lemons and combine zest and juice
with rest of dressing ingredients. Toss with shredded cabbage, fennel,
thinly sliced apples and cranberries and let sit about half an hour
before serving to allow the flavours to come together.

Salad

1 medium head cabbage
(green, red or both)

1 fennel bulb,
greens attached

2 apples

½ cup dried cranberries

Dressing

1½ cups yogurt

3 tbsp honey

2 to 3 lemons

People who have invested time and energy in mastering a craft are a real wellspring of inspiration and joy for me as a chef—whether they're creating artisanal salt, pottery, or natural wine, or raising chickens. The idea of "maker" culture has become quite a trend, but for me it's much more than that.

about MAKERS

WHEN PHILIPPE, our salt maker, comes to the door and hands me the fresh salt crystals he's made, there's this moment of mutual appreciation and love that passes between us. For me, I'm grateful for this gift he's brought, and I'm excited because it's going to take my dishes to the next level. My family and our guests on the farm are going to have a better experience of their food because of what he has created. Philippe—who has invested himself in this salt, and made it something really lovely—knows that I value what he does. I see it, and honour it, and he feels that and is grateful. It's a kind of moment that is difficult to get in a supermarket.

It might be Meghan coming in with beet thinnings from the plants she's grown from seed, or visiting our regional cheesemakers and winemakers, or the pottery maker bringing us freshly fired plates and bowls. With each meeting there's a feeling of love and appreciation, a short but deep dive into our mutual connection to things we enjoy, to the Earth, and to each other.

The first kitchen knife I ever fell in love with was made by a very special friend of ours, Seth Burton, who is the creator of Cosmo Knives here on Salt Spring Island. In the years since, I have collected more of Seth's knives. As I have grown as a chef, Seth has grown as a master knife maker and bladesmith. I am honoured to call him a friend and have the beauty of his knives grace my kitchen.

I'd like the things in my kitchen and home—my salt, my olive oil, my plates, even my silverware (I am determined to forge my own fork one day!)—to be from people who crafted them with care, even if I can't meet them all.

When your home is full of things that have true soul and love in them, people can feel it. The food looks better. It tastes better. The whole experience is more nourishing.

This is an old French picnic dish—it's traditionally served at room temperature, but I often serve it warm as a dinner entrée. Adults and kids love it for the wonderful combination of sweet and savoury. SERVES 4 TO 6

chicken MARBELLA

The key to this dish is starting with a good-quality whole free-range chicken, ensuring excellent flavour. Pre-cut thighs or breasts work as well. Traditionally prunes and olives are tucked around the chicken, but I like to change the fruit with the seasons, like early apples or fresh plums in the summer. I've also started using quince in the autumn with really beautiful results. If you're pairing with wine, a good merlot really complements the Mediterranean herbs and the sweetness of the dried plums.

Heat oven to 375°F. Place cut-up chicken in 9 × 12-inch baking pan. Cut prunes or plums in half and remove any pits. Pour wine and olive oil over the chicken. Sprinkle remaining ingredients overtop, pressing olives and prunes down in between the chicken pieces. Bake for approximately 1 hour, until golden brown.

1 free-range chicken (about 3 to 5 lb)

2 cups white wine

¼ cup extra-virgin olive oil

¼ cup brown sugar

2 tbsp dried oregano

1 cup prunes or fresh plums

1 cup Sicilian olives

Each year on the farm we grow a big crop of Yukon gold potatoes to store for the winter, enough to supply all of the families here until early spring. With this recipe, you're pre-cooking the potatoes—a technique used a lot around the Mediterranean—and then tossing them with olive oil into a nice, hot oven. They turn out perfectly crispy and delicious. They make an excellent side with chicken, salmon or any juicy winter roast (or served reheated the next day as hash browns). Once you try them you'll never want roasted potatoes any other way. SERVES 4 TO 6

perfect crispy POTATOES

4 lb potatoes

1 tsp + 1½ tsp salt

3 tbsp extra-virgin olive oil

Heat oven to 425°F and line a baking tray with parchment paper. Wash the potatoes—if organic, leave peels on. Cut into pieces roughly 2 inches square. Place cut potatoes into a pot and cover with about two inches of water. Add 1 tsp salt. Bring to a boil and cook until just tender, about 10 to 15 minutes. Drain well.

In a large bowl, toss potatoes with olive oil and remaining 1½ tsp salt, and spread on a baking tray. Roast for about 45 minutes, until golden and crispy, stirring gently partway through.

This gratin is a real comfort-food dish, similar to scalloped potatoes but with butternut squash adding a touch of sweetness and the goat cheese adding a layer of rich, creamy flavour. Baked until golden and bubbling, it makes a wonderful side dish any time of year. In deep winter it makes a lovely dinner on its own with a hearty salad and a cold glass of chablis with good, crisp minerality. SERVES 6 TO 8

yukon gold potato, squash and GOAT CHEESE GRATIN

Heat oven to 400°F and butter a 9 × 12-inch baking dish. Thinly slice unpeeled potatoes in rounds. Peel, seed and thinly slice squash in large, half-moon pieces. Mince fresh thyme and set aside.

Layer potatoes and squash in baking dish. Pour heavy cream and sprinkle salt evenly over everything. Cream should reach to the top layer of the sliced potatoes and squash. Crumble cheese and sprinkle over squash and potatoes along with fresh thyme.

Bake in oven for approximately 1 hour, until golden and bubbling and potatoes and squash are tender when pierced with a fork.

10 to 12 medium-sized Yukon gold potatoes (about 2 lb)

2 lb butternut squash

8 oz chèvre (about 1 cup)

3 to 4 cups heavy cream

2 tsp salt

2 tbsp fresh thyme or 1 tbsp dried

As with pastry, scones have a reputation of being tricky to make, but after a few batches they become easy. They say you can have "pastry hands" (or, in the American South, "biscuit hands")—but rather than being born with or without them and being fated to succeed or fail, the meaning is more about the art of working with pastry or dough. The secret is to work the dough quickly without allowing your hands to warm up the butter in the dough. If the butter melts, you lose the flakiness. You want the butter to stay cold once it's mixed with the flour, so pastry hands are all about working quickly and lightly. MAKES ABOUT 10 SCONES

scones

3 cups unbleached
white flour

¼ cup sugar

2½ tsp baking powder

½ tsp baking soda

½ tsp salt

1¾ sticks cold
unsalted butter

1 cup buttermilk
(or 1 cup milk + 1 tsp vinegar)

Grated zest of 1 lemon or orange

2 tbsp sugar for
sprinkling on scones

1 cup currants or dried
cranberries (optional)

This recipe is based on Julia Child's beautiful scones, a recipe I've used for many years. These scones are so wonderful to make first thing on a weekend morning when the sun is shining through the kitchen windows. Throw your currants and lemon zest in there and you get bright, beautiful flavours to liven up your morning. Delicious served warm out of the oven with butter and preserves—or packed for picnics and school lunches.

Heat oven to 425°F. Cut 1½ sticks of butter into small pieces, reserving ¼ stick. In bowl of stand mixer or food processor, mix together flour, sugar, baking powder, baking soda and salt. Add butter pieces and mix or pulse briefly until mixture resembles coarse cornmeal. You want some butter pieces to remain a little bigger as this helps give the scones flakiness.

Add buttermilk, zest and optional currants or cranberries. Mix briefly until dough is just starting to hold together. Turn dough out onto a lightly floured counter. Gather dough into a ball, pressing gently together with your hands. Knead very briefly, until holding together well. Cut dough in half. Roll out each piece into a circle about 6 inches across.

Melt remaining ¼ stick of butter. Brush dough with melted butter and sprinkle with sugar. Cut each circle into 6 equal triangles, and transfer to a parchment-lined baking tray. Bake on top rack of oven for 10 to 12 minutes, until golden brown on top and bottom. Transfer to a rack to cool.

This cheesecake really shines when made with high-quality, fresh chèvre. There are many artisanal, small-batch cheese makers who produce fantastic fresh cheeses. The lightness and purity of this cheesecake make it a very special dessert. SERVES 6 TO 8

fresh chèvre CHEESECAKE

For the flour, a whole-wheat variety such as red fife would add a nice nutty flavour; you can also use your favourite gluten-free blend.

Heat oven to 375°F and butter a 10-inch springform pan. Combine flour, ⅓ cup sugar, butter and salt in a medium-sized bowl. Mix until thoroughly combined. Press into bottom of springform pan, coming up the inside edge about 2 inches. Bake for 12 to 15 minutes, until golden brown.

   With electric mixer on medium, whip heavy cream until soft peaks form. Set aside.

   With mixer on medium-high, mix chèvre, sugar and vanilla together until light and fluffy (about 3 minutes). Using a spatula, gently and thoroughly fold whipped cream into chèvre mixture. Spread into prepared crust. Refrigerate for at least 1 hour before serving. Serve on its own or with fresh berries.

28 oz fresh chèvre
(about 4 cups)

1 cup + ⅓ cup fine white sugar

1½ cups heavy cream

2 tsp vanilla

2 cups unbleached white flour

⅔ cup butter, room temperature

½ tsp salt

2 cups fresh berries
(optional)

ACKNOWLEDGMENTS

THIS FARM WOULD not be what it is without the land. We would like to acknowledge the ancestral, traditional and unceded Aboriginal territories of the Coast Salish People whose territory we are on. We are grateful to this land and all the creatures, big and small, with whom we share it. We are thankful for the lake—we appreciate you for your cleansing energy and the life you bring.

There have been many people who have helped, encouraged, and supported us in the long road of getting this book published, and we are grateful for all of you: Marlyn Horsdal, Nadine Shelley, Kirsty Smythe, Karen LeBillon, Ron Watts, Syd Woodward & Hemmie Lindholm. Thank you for your time and being willing to do some veggie trades along the way.

A huge, warm thank you to Tyee Bridge of Arclight Media. We appreciate you seeing us, believing in us and bringing patience, humour and focus to our many times together. Thank you for being willing to edit this book anywhere, even on a remote boat on the West Coast. You truly have been a blessing.

We are so grateful to have worked with Page Two Strategies, especially Jesse Finkelstein, Peter Cocking and Rony Ganon. Your ongoing support, encouragement and expertise have made it all possible. We will definitely be sharing more delicious food in the future.

Thank you to Rush Jagoe, our photographer extraordinaire, for being so fun to work with, for integrating into our lives and capturing this place so perfectly.

We are so lucky to have had Zoe Grams as part of our team—thank you, Zoe, for your enthusiasm in getting our book out into the world.

We are grateful to Michael Ableman for not only generously agreeing to write the foreword, but also for the ongoing inspiration you have brought to us as small-scale organic farmers.

Jennifer, Liz, and Haidee wish to thank Lisa, from the bottom of their hearts, for this opportunity, for all your patience, wisdom and love, and for putting up with us. We love you!

We also offer our gratitude to:

Our families—husbands, children, parents, mothers- and fathers-in-law—all of you who have loved us and supported our process along the way.

David Karr for support to get this book off the ground.

Anne, Sarah, and Amrei for testing all the recipes so carefully and thoroughly.

Dan Jason, for supporting and inspiring our seed-saving operation and witnessing our farm grow into what it has become.

The farming community on Salt Spring Island for all your personality, community and tenacity. We hope to share many more potlucks with you all.

All the weeders, pea pickers, and compost movers. This farm has been cared for by many hardworking farming folks like you, and we acknowledge the farmers, permaculture specialists, wwoofers, apprentices and other volunteers who have spent days, months, and years in the garden helping shape it into the farm we have today.

All the teachers who have taught classes over the years in Lisa's house, in the Barn and in the Gatehouse. It was through these classes and your teachings that we began to develop retreats on the farm.

A special mention here to Heather Martin for teaching yoga in the old house and to the original group of meditators who used to sit on Lisa's porch, paving the way for future retreats.

The verandah of the old house and all the community members it held, especially during strawberry season.

The Reynolds Road community for everything, including shaking it up at the Barn dances.

The Reynolds family for homesteading and the Byrons for being great neighbours.

All the people who lived on the farm in the early years, in school buses, tipis, yurts and cabins, and who contributed in so many ways to the unfolding of our community.

Roog for years of friendship, support, advice and humour.

Stuart Lloyd for having the vision to buy this place with Lisa in the beginning and for your interest and love.

All the people who work here in the various and important ways, tending gardens, teaching children, taking care of our bookkeeping: you are all integral to this place.

The carpenters, woodworkers, and craftspeople who have built beauty into this place through the buildings, decks, docks and houses. We so appreciate your skill and all the energy that you have put into the farm, especially Dewey Snetsinger, Doug Motherwell, Mark Vanderwerf, Doug Rhodes, Tom Reigle, Andrew Currie, Luke Hart-Weller, Joshua Hart, Robert Moss and Michael Dragland.

The yogis, meditators, dancers, soul searchers, nature connectors, silent ones, noisy ones, rebar benders, song catchers, animal trackers, and musicians who have come here on retreat or otherwise. Without you coming to the farm we wouldn't be what we are.

Amy Caesar for starting the yurt primary education program.

Thank you so much to Amrei Hunter for being Haidee's sous chef extraordinaire and bringing so much talent, love and beauty to the farm kitchen.

We are part of the incredible community of Salt Spring Island and we want to thank you for supporting us in all the ways you do: buying veggies, coming to classes, attending retreats, giving advice, sharing yourselves with us. We couldn't do what we do without you.

We also want to acknowledge the people who are leading the movements that we're a part of—the radical and small-scale organic farmers, the slow-foodies, the slow-musicians, the permaculturalists, the back-to-the-landers/homesteaders, the herbalists, the off-the-grid folks, the crafty-maker folk.

To work on this book we had to get off the farm. We had a few favourite places that were key to bringing this work to life. Alix Brown's place in Vancouver: we can't think of a better place to be in the city. To Janet and Saint for Ch-ahayis on Chesterman's Beach: we love the hours we spent there talking, writing and walking the beach. And to the very memorable Innchanter—thank you, Shaun, and the hotsprings—what a place to vision a book!

We would like to thank Guayakí for your vision and inspiration that have bolstered our lives here on the farm.

Nothing would have been the same without Garry Kaye who farmed in the very early days with Lisa. Thank you for your kindness, consistency and hard work. Without you those years would not have been possible. And to Bly and Graham who, with Garry, have been our cherished and long-time neighbours.

And thanks to all of our other allies and friends, you know who you are: H H, Daphne Taylor, Julie Kimmel, Amy Cousins, Rachel Bevington, Evelyne & David, Shani Cranston, Alinka Porebska, Celeste Mallett-Jason, Gay Young, Cathy Valentine, Alice Friedman, Dorothy Price, Kathe Faraci, Tara Martin, Ramona & Brendan, Paul Shoebridge, Nettie Wild, Mika Senda, Michael Nickels, Heidi Cowan, Brandon Bauer, Jamie & Angela, Pat Byron, Mark Hughes, Anne Macy, Ingrid & Jean-Claude, Christo Munneke, Sharon & Doug, Tanis & Nick, Kirsty, April Roach, all the trades people.

The Stowel Lake Farm 'farmies': Milo, Adam & Aneta, Matt, David, Josh, Roman, Meghan, Thea, Nicola, Honor, Lenka, Pato, Ashley, and Josephine; and all the children who bring such joy to all of our lives: Aliah, Noah, Jacob, Atisha, Hanna, Addie, Alex, Aurelia, Max, India, Rio, Alden, and Scout.

about the AUTHORS

Lisa Lloyd is the founder of Stowel Lake Farm. She moved to the farm in 1979 with her three children, Rachel, Hamish and Jennifer, and has lived here ever since. Along with helping oversee the life of the farm, she is an avid gardener, a student of permaculture and a lover of swallows. When she can get off the farm she loves travelling, especially extended kayak trips in the wilderness.

Jennifer Lloyd-Karr has lived on Stowel Lake Farm (with a few breaks for university, travel and guiding work) since she was five years old. She loves dancing, healthy living and family sailing trips off BC's west coast. In the winter months you might find Jen longboarding in warmer oceans. She facilitates the community and co-manages business operations on the farm, where she lives with her husband, David, and their sons, Alex and Rio.

Elizabeth Young moved to Stowel Lake Farm in 2000. After living in a school bus and a yurt, she built a house here with her husband, Matt, where they are raising their three children, Addie, Maxwell and Scout. Liz also loves surfing (with Jennifer), forest walks and singing with others. She co-facilitates the farm business and community, and teaches yoga in the Gatehouse.

Haidee Hart has lived on Stowel Lake Farm with her husband, Josh, since 2005. Their four children—Aliah, Noah, Jacob and India—have all grown up here. The chef for the farm, she is passionate about farm-to-table food, natural wines and foraging for wild ingredients with camera in hand. Haidee and her family spend part of the year in Australia, where they love exploring the hinterland and the wild coastal areas. Return guests look forward to seeing Haidee's welcoming smile in the kitchen.